Effective
Adoption
Panels

Guidance on regulations, process
and good practice in adoption and
permanence panels in England

Jenifer Lord
Deborah Cullen

Published by
British Association for Adoption
& Fostering
BAAF
Saffron House
6–10 Kirby Street
London EC1N 8TS
www.baaf.org.uk

Charity registration 275689 (England and Wales)
and SC039337 (Scotland)

© BAAF 1997, 2000, 2006, 2009, 2012
Second edition 2000
Third edition 2006
Fourth edition 2009
Fifth edition 2012

British Library Cataloguing in Publication Data
A catalogue record for this book is available from the
British Library

ISBN 978 1 907585 32 6

Project management by Shaila Shah, Director of
Publications, BAAF
Designed and typeset by Helen Joubert Design
Printed in Great Britain by The Lavenham Press

BAAF is the leading UK-wide membership
organisation for all those concerned with adoption,
fostering and child care issues.

Contents

Acknowledgements   vii

Notes about the authors   vii

Introduction   1

Current regulations and guidance   1

How this guide will help you   2

How this guide is structured   2

Using this guide   3

Appendices   3

1 Establishing the panel   4

Requirement to have an adoption panel   4

Membership of an adoption panel –
the regulations   4

Membership of a joint adoption panel   4

Frequency of panel meetings   4

Membership – practice issues   4

The central list   5

Appointment to sit on a panel   5

Chair   5

Social work members   6

Elected members (local authority) or director,
manager or other officer of a voluntary adoption
agency   6

Medical adviser   7

Independent panel members   7

Vice-Chair   7

Agency adviser to the panel   7

Legal advice   8

Attendance of non-panel members at panel
meetings   8

Quorum   9

Appointment of substitutes   9

Recruitment   9

Central list and panel membership agreement   10

Checks on central list and panel members   10

Induction and training   11

Review of central list and panel members   11

Adoption panel fees   12

Tenure of office of members of the central list
and adoption panel   12

Resignation by central list and panel members   12

Termination of appointment of central list and
panel members   12

Adoption panel functions   13

Adoption and permanence panel   13

Adoption reports   14

Declaring an interest   15

Reaching a recommendation   15

The decision-maker   16

Agency decision-making   16

Administration   16

Disclosure of minutes   18

Monitoring and review   18

Adoption inspection   19

2 Agency policy and practice issues   20

Making the adoption process work well   20

Duties in relation to adoption   20

The "welfare checklist" in relation to adoption   20

Achieving good policies and practice in adoption
work   21

Adoption panel policies and procedures   22

The panel's involvement in contributing to
good practice   22

Specific issues which panel members will need
to consider   22

Family structures   23

References   23

Criminal background   24

Health and disability issues   24

Lesbian and gay issues   25

Discipline issues		25
Matching policy in relation to culture, "race", religion and language		26
Permanence		26
Contact		26
Health and safety issues		26
Financial matters		26
Family work patterns		26
Adoption support services		27
Placements with family members or existing foster carers		27
Members of staff		27
Duration of approval		27
Representations and complaints		28

3 Considering adoption for a child   29

Introduction		29
The range of children considered by the panel		29
Panel functions		30
Timescales		30
Information required		30
Legal advice		31
People attending the panel		31
Welfare of children		31
The child's permanence report		31
Issues to consider		32
Permanence options		35
Practice considerations in relation to permanence options		36
Contact issues		36
Giving advice on whether a placement order should be applied for		37
Conditional or "in principle" recommendations		37
Minutes		38
What next?		38

4 Families offering placements   40

Introduction		40
Function of the panel		40
The range of families available		40
Timescales		41
Information required for a full report		41
Checks and references required		42
The full prospective adopter's report		43
Legal advice		44
Conditional or "in principle" recommendations		44
Brief report		44
Applicants attending the panel		44
Issues to consider		45
Preparation, training and support		45
Strengths needed		46
Issues relating to the family		46
Issues relating to meeting the child's needs		47
Range of approval		49
Decision-making process		49
Review and termination of approval		50
What next?		50

5 Matching children with families   52

Panel functions		52
Process by which the proposed match has reached the panel		52
Timescales		53
Authorisation to place for adoption		53
Information required		53
Legal advice		54
Attendance at the panel		54
Welfare of children		55
Issues to consider		55
Adoption support services		57
Contact arrangements		58

Parental responsibility 58

Baby placements where the child is
relinquished for adoption 59

Reaching a recommendation on a proposed
match 59

What next? 59

6 Intercountry adoption 61

Introduction 61

Agency policies and procedures 61

Considering and deciding whether a child should
be placed for adoption outside the British Islands 61

Considering whether a child should be placed
for adoption in a Hague Convention country 62

The panel's involvement in considering a
match with approved adopters from a Hague
Convention country 63

The panel's involvement in children's cases
when the Hague Convention is not in force in
the overseas country 64

Considering prospective adopters 64

Issues relating to the family 64

Change of approval 66

Post-placement and post-adoption support 66

Appendix 1: Context of the agency's
placement work 67

Appendix 2: Acts of Parliament, Statutory
Instruments and Government Guidance 69

Appendix 3: Glossary of terms 70

Appendix 4: Useful organisations 74

Introduction to Adoption:
National Minimum Standards 2011 77

Sample job description and person
specification for central list and panel
members 78

Review of central list and panel members 80

Sample self-evaluation form:
Central list and panel member 81

Sample review form:
central list and panel members 83

Sample job description and person
specification for panel Chair 84

Review of panel Chair 86

Sample self-evaluation form: Panel Chair 87

Sample review form: panel Chair 89

Checklist of additional information
which may be provided by the agency 90

Book list 91

Acknowledgements

The original edition of *Effective Panels*, published in 1997, drew on the experience and expertise of members of a working party. Others with personal or professional experience of adoption were also consulted and all were acknowledged in the original and subsequent editions. This edition also draws on the wisdom of these individuals, and we would like to thank them again.

Jenifer Lord would also like to acknowledge and thank everyone involved with the adoption and permanence panels in Southampton, Brent and Harrow. She has learnt a huge amount from her participation in these panels.

Notes about the authors

Jenifer Lord was a Child Placement Consultant for BAAF Southern England. She has chaired an adoption panel, and is currently a member of another one. She is also the author of *Adopting a Child* and *The Adoption Process*, and co-author of *Effective Fostering Panels*.

Deborah Cullen was the Legal Group Co-ordinator at BAAF. She has authored several articles and books on child care law.

Introduction

All adoption agencies, both local authority and voluntary, have been required to have adoption panels since the Adoption Agencies Regulations 1983 came into force in 1984. From December 30 2005, when the Adoption and Children Act 2002 was implemented in full, new regulations replaced these.

Current regulations and guidance

The principal regulations governing adoption work in England are the Adoption Agencies Regulations 2005. However, new regulations, the **Adoption Agencies and Independent Review of Determinations (Amendment) Regulations 2011** replace Regulations 3 to 10 of the Adoption Agencies Regulations 2005, as amended, from 1 April 2011. These eight regulations are the ones covering panels. There is also revised **statutory Adoption Guidance**, issued in February 2011 and further amended in late April 2011. New **National Minimum Standards for Adoption** were issued in 2011. These, and other relevant sets of regulations, are listed in Appendix II. Reference is made to the statutory Guidance, by chapter number and section (for example, Chapter 3 section 29 is 3.29).In addition, reference is made to the National Minimum Adoption Standards as NMS and the standard number. The regulations are referred to, in the main, by their initials (see list in Appendix 2), although the new regulations dealing with panels are just referred to as, e.g. regulation 2.

Although the new regulations and guidance make a significant number of changes, the basic composition and functions of panels remain largely the same as before. Each aspect of the agency's adoption work – making adoption plans for children, considering the suitability of prospective adopters and matching individual children with adoptive parents – must be considered by the panel and the panel's recommendation must be taken into account by the agency when making its decision.

A major change is that panels no longer have a fixed membership. Instead, agencies must establish a **central list** of people from which the membership

of the panel, each time it meets, is chosen. In practice, many agencies have established a core group of panel members from the central list who attend most panel meetings, with other central list members attending from time to time. The same chairperson, who must be independent of the agency, will usually be appointed to each panel. There must be at least one social worker present and there will often be a medical adviser and usually a number of independent members who are likely to include an adoptive parent and an adopted adult. This diverse group of people, pooling and sharing their different experience and expertise, can speak from a very informed perspective and with an authoritative voice, providing a vital scrutiny as well as a validation of the agency's work.

Over the years panels have changed and developed in the way they work. Many now consider children for whom long-term fostering is the proposed plan as well as those for whom adoption is the plan. Prospective adopters must now be invited to attend panel when their approval is being considered. Many agencies also invite them to attend when a match with them is being considered. Making sure that the views of birth parents and of the child are made clearly known to the panel is an essential consideration too.

Effective Adoption Panels acknowledges the vital role which panels play in relation to children needing adoption, their birth families, and their adoptive parents and foster carers. It aims to help panels to make sound and effective recommendations. Panels have an extremely important role to play within agencies and are expected to provide expert advice to adoption agencies, and to contribute to the development of policies and procedures.

Their key role is:

- to provide an independent scrutiny of the proposals presented and to determine
    - whether all the issues have been appropriately clarified; and
    - whether the proposal is sound.

How this guide will help you

This guide will be of interest and value not only to new and existing central list and panel members in England but also to all those who come into contact with the work of panels, particularly social workers, agency managers, committee members, adoptive parents and foster carers, and a wide range of other professionals.

For central list and panel members themselves the key aims of this guide are:

- to inform them about their roles and responsibilities;

- to update them on current legislation and issues of good practice;

- to help them integrate this work within their own agency context and policies;

- to equip them with the knowledge, understanding and confidence needed to make appropriate recommendations in the best interests of children;

- to encourage them to play a full role as individual panel members and to continue to learn more about this task.

It is essential that panel members are also given opportunities for regular training. It is hoped that the guide will alert agency staff and panel members to some of the issues which it would be helpful to cover more fully in training sessions.

How this guide is structured

We have organised this guide into six chapters followed by appendices.

Establishing the panel describes the range of cases which the panel may deal with, the central list and panel membership, and the role of each member. It outlines the terms and conditions of membership and the process for reaching a recommendation on individual cases. The panel's wider role and the importance of good administration and training are also discussed.

Agency policy and practice issues considers the panel's role in helping the agency draw up policies and procedures for adoption work within the context of the agency's wider work. It also describes specific issues which the panel will need to consider and on which clear policies or practice guidance may

be useful. Current good practice and findings from research are described.

Considering adoption for a child Considering whether adoption is the best plan for a child is one of the tasks of the panel. This chapter describes the range of factors which panel members will need to take into account before reaching their recommendation. It alerts them to the importance of checking on the progress of work with and on behalf of the child once the adoption plan has been agreed. There is a flow chart which sets out what will have happened before the case comes to the panel.

Families offering placements describes the issues which the panel will need to consider and take into account before making its recommendation as to whether an applicant is suitable to be an adoptive parent. It describes the Independent Review Mechanism (IRM). It also alerts panel members to the importance of reviewing the situation of waiting approved applicants. A flow chart sets out the stages in the process of work with families, both before and after the panel's recommendation.

Matching children and families describes the different ways in which matches may be made. It outlines the range of factors which panel members will need to consider before making a recommendation on whether a prospective adopter would be a suitable adoptive parent for a particular child. It also alerts panel members to the importance of receiving information on and of reviewing placements which have been made. A flow chart sets out what will have happened before the match comes to the panel.

Intercountry adoption Many, although not all, panels will consider the cases of families who are hoping to adopt from overseas. This chapter describes the process of intercountry adoption and the particular and different role of the panel in these cases. Panel members are alerted to the particular issues which they should consider, over and above those which they would consider in domestic adoption cases. For the first time, panels also have a role in considering whether a looked after child should be placed for adoption overseas and in considering a match, and issues involved in these considerations are described.

Using this guide

Effective Adoption Panels is designed both to be read from start to finish and also to be dipped into as particular issues arise. To enable readers to follow up issues more fully, each chapter includes cross-references to other chapters and ends with a list of references to research findings. Many of the books and articles mentioned are published by BAAF and are easily available.

A list of all the Acts, Regulations and Guidance and Standards mentioned is provided in Appendix 2. Each agency will have copies of these, and many of them can be downloaded from the Department for Education website at www.education.gov.uk.

Useful organisations are also listed in the appendices as is a glossary of terms. Throughout this guide, the term "children" refers to both children and young people. Similarly, we have used the term "applicants" to refer to prospective adopters who could be single, married, or in a partnership.

Appendices

The appendices of this book contain some supplementary information that agencies will find useful. This includes:

- Context of the agency's placement work

- Values statement which underpins the National Minimum Standards for Adoption

- Sample job description and person specification for the Chair

- Sample job description and person specification for central list and panel members

- Sample review format for the Chair

- Sample review format for central list and panel members

- Checklist for additional information

- A list of useful books for further reading.

Your agency may wish to use the job descriptions, person specifications and review formats that we have provided, or adapt them, or use their own material.

A pocket has been provided on the inside back cover, and we hope that you will use this to store other relevant information obtainable from the agency, as advised in this guide.

1 Establishing the panel

Requirement to have an adoption panel

Regulation 4 (1) requires that 'the adoption agency must constitute one or more adoption panels, as necessary'.

Regulation 4 (3) allows, as previously, that 'any two or more local authorities may jointly constitute an adoption panel'.

As previously, there is no provision for voluntary adoption agencies (VAA) to establish joint panels. However, Guidance 1.34 states that different branches of the same VAA may share a panel.

Membership of an adoption panel – the regulations

Regulation 3 states that the agency 'must maintain a list of persons who are considered by it to be suitable to be members of an adoption panel ('the central list')'. Included on it must be:

- one or more social workers who have at least three years' relevant post-qualifying experience;

- the medical adviser to the adoption agency (or at least one if more than one medical adviser is appointed).

Regulation 4 requires that the agency must appoint from the central list:

- a person to chair the panel, who is independent of the agency;

- one or two people as vice-chairs, who may act as Chair, if necessary.

Regulation 6 requires that no business may be conducted unless the following meet as a panel:

- the Chair or one of the Vice-chairs;

- a social worker, as defined in Regulation 3;

- three (or for a joint panel, four) other members. If the Chair is not present and the Vice-chair is not independent, then at least one other panel member must be an independent person.

Membership of a joint adoption panel

There is no difference between a joint panel and a single one except that the membership must be agreed by the agencies and the quorum must include four rather than three "other members", making a total of six members. Agencies will probably share a central list of potential panel members. Guidance on joint panels is given in 1.34.

Frequency of panel meetings

There is guidance on this in 1.25: 'Adoption panels must not be the "bottleneck" in the decision-making process. They must meet frequently and be able to meet at short notice before the next scheduled meeting to deal with urgent cases.' NMS 17.3 specifies that adoption panels should meet at least monthly unless it is an adoption panel of a small voluntary adoption agency, when it should meet six-weekly.

Membership – practice issues

Panels do not have a fixed membership or a maximum number of members. Guidance 1.27 states that: 'Each agency must maintain a list of persons whom it considers suitable to be members of an adoption panel. There is no limit to the number of people who may be included on the central list.' Guidance 1.41 requires that: 'When constituting an adoption panel the agency must draw members from the central list. These members must have the appropriate qualifications and/or experience to consider the cases submitted to the adoption panel.' The same people do not need to be appointed to every panel meeting. Subject to each meeting being quorate, Guidance 1.41 states: 'It is for the agency to decide how many panel members should be present at each panel meeting. However, a panel should not be so large as to make it difficult to chair the meeting or intimidating for those attending the meeting.'

Possibly a greater concern is that the panel may only ever be just quorate with not more than the required number of people being appointed to make it so. It would be particularly unfortunate if this resulted in the independent service user experience and expertise being diminished.

The central list

As described in more detail elsewhere in this chapter, all persons on the central list must have full checks, must be given induction and training, and must have a written panel agreement and an annual review of their performance. Although there is no limit to the number of people on the list, it is likely to work best, both from the agency's and the person's point of view, if it is small enough to give everyone the opportunity to be involved with the agency and to be invited on a regular basis to attend panel. There is no tenure requirement but, as discussed in the section on tenure, it will be important to ensure that new members are added to the list from time to time. In order for the list not to become unmanageably large, this will mean people coming off the list from time to time. There is no formal guidance on there being a diverse group of people on the central list or panel, but this would be good practice. There is also no formal guidance on "reflecting the community", although again this would be good practice.

Appointment to sit on a panel

Guidance 1.27 states that: 'Having a pool of people with different skills, experience and qualifications allows for the most appropriate members to be drawn upon to consider individual cases and reduces the likelihood of panel meetings having to be postponed, whilst retaining knowledgeable and experienced members without the need for a vacancy to occur to appoint a new member to the list.'

There is no requirement to have a fixed membership on panel. However, as stated in the guidance for fostering panels, which are set up in the same way, 'the ability of the panel to function cohesively and with a level of consistency must be taken into account. This may be best achieved by having at least a core membership'. Experience suggests that the panel is likely to function best if most members know each other and are used to working as a group. Cases often recur with people approved to adopt subsequently coming back to panel to be matched with a child, whose plan the panel has considered. It can be helpful if the same panel

members are involved in these considerations. Agencies should have written procedures on how and by whom decisions are made about who to appoint to a particular panel. It is important that this is seen to be transparent, fair and consistent.

Chair

The requirement to appoint an independent Chair from the central list to chair the panel is in Regulation 4. A person is not independent if they are:

- in the case of a registered adoption society, a trustee or employee of that society;
- in the case of a local authority:
  - an elected member of that authority; or
  - employed by that authority in the adoption service or for the purposes of any of that local authority's functions relating to the protection or placement of children;
- in either case, the adoptive parent of a child placed by that agency or an adoptive parent approved by that agency, even if the child is placed by another agency, unless at least 12 months have elapsed since an adoption order was made in respect of the child.

Regulation 4 specifies that the Chair must have the 'skills and experience' necessary to chair. Guidance 1.29 details the most significant qualities as being:

- 'a sound understanding of the adoption process;
- the authority and competence to chair a panel;
- the ability to analyse and explain complex information;
- the ability to identify key issues, problems and solutions;
- excellent interpersonal, oral and written communication skills.'

The Guidance continues that if the Chair does not possess 'a sound understanding of the adoption process but possesses all the other qualities, they may be appointed provided the agency considers that they will quickly develop an understanding of the adoption process and the agency ensures that the panel Chair receives appropriate training before taking up their appointment.'

- Guidance details key aspects of the Chair's role. He or she

  - should make it clear that every member's view is as valid as others, and should encourage everyone to participate and contribute to the panel's recommendations (Guidance 1.43);

  - is responsible for ensuring the accuracy of the panel's recommendations, reasons and, following agreement with panel members, the minutes (Guidance 1.44);

  - must make sure that a person who is not a member of the panel fulfils the task of writing these documents (Guidance 1.44).

- Where panel members have serious reservations, the Chair must ensure these are recorded in the minutes and are attached to the panel's recommendation (Guidance 1.4).

- If the panel cannot reach a consensus on its recommendation after the Chair and other panel members have voted, the panel Chair has a second vote, i.e. the casting vote (Guidance 1.45).

- It is important for the Chair to remind social workers and attending applicants that the panel makes a recommendation and not a decision and to give a time-frame for the agency decision.

- The panel Chair has a responsibility, with the agency adviser to the panel, to review annually the performance of all central list and panel members (Guidance 1.35).

- Linked to the review, the Chair should have a role in the appointment and induction of new central list members and in any consideration about terminating the appointment of a member.

- The Chair has a gatekeeping role in relation to papers coming to panel: 'Where there are concerns about a report, the agency adviser and the panel Chair should consider whether it is adequate for submission to panel' (Guidance 1.32).

- Regulation 19(2) makes clear that 'no member of the adoption panel shall take part in any decision made by the adoption agency'. This suggests that a meeting after each panel between the Chair and the decision-maker is probably not good practice. If a meeting is needed, it may be more appropriate for the agency adviser to be involved. However, a regular meeting, perhaps every six months, to discuss general issues, could be very useful.

Other responsibilities of the Chair are likely to be:

- involvement in decisions on the attendance of observers at panel;

- involvement when a panel member declares an interest in a case;

- involvement in deciding when an extra panel may need to be convened to consider an urgent case;

- involvement in the preparation of an annual report on the panel's work.

The Chair's crucial role in chairing panel meetings and in facilitating the making of well thought through and evidenced recommendations is described in the later section, *Reaching a recommendation*.

Their shared role, with the agency adviser, in the annual review of panel members is described in the later section, *Review of panel members*.

The Chair has particular responsibilities and requires particular skills. It is likely to work best if he or she is appointed on a regular basis to chair an agency's panel and to carry out other tasks, such as the annual review of central list members. However, it would be possible for an agency to have several people on its central list who have the experience and skills needed to chair a panel.

Social work members

Regulation 3(i)(a) requires the agency to include on its central list 'one or more social workers who have at least three years' relevant post-qualifying experience'. Guidance 1.29 specifies that this should be 'in child care social work, including direct experience in adoption work'. This could involve having worked with adopters or with a child being placed for adoption. The social workers do not need to be employed by the agency.

Elected members (local authority) or director, manager or other officer of a voluntary adoption agency

There is no requirement to have someone in this role on the central list of potential panel members. However, as representatives of the corporate parent, a local authority elected member may make a valuable contribution as a central list and panel member.

Panel members in this role need to be aware of and sensitive to the potential power dynamics between themselves and social workers from that agency who may be fellow panel members or may be presenting cases to panel.

Medical adviser

Regulation 3(1)(b) requires an agency to include on its central list the medical adviser to the adoption agency (or at least one if more than one medical adviser is appointed). Although the medical adviser is not necessary for the panel to be quorate and is not required to be appointed to the panel, their presence can be very helpful and it may be a good idea if the agency has more than one medical adviser whom it can appoint to sit on a panel.

Unlike other panel members, the medical adviser also contributes to the paperwork considered by panel. He or she is required to write a summary on the child's health which forms part of the child's permanence report (AAR 17(1)(b)), and a summary on the prospective adopter's health which forms part of their report for panel (AAR 25(5)(b)). The medical adviser should also be consulted when the agency prepares the adoption placement report about a match for panel (Guidance 1.8). The medical adviser will be able to add verbally to their written report and to answer questions on health issues at the request of other panel members.

It is recommended in Guidance 1.8 that the agency 'make arrangements for the appointment of its medical adviser with a local Primary Care Trust's designated doctor for looked after children'.

Independent panel members

Each panel must have an independent Chair. There is no requirement for other independent panel members although if the Chair is unable to be present, there needs to be at least one independent Vice-chair or, failing that, another independent panel member. Independence is defined in the same way as for the panel Chair. Guidance 1.19 states that panels 'are intended to be multi-disciplinary bodies with a considerable element of independence from the agency'. Guidance 1.29 suggests that 'suitable members could include specialists in education,

child and adolescent mental health, race and culture; and those who have personal experience of adoption'. The adoption panel has an important role in providing independent scrutiny of the work of the agency in relation to the cases presented to it. Panels as constituted up to now have benefited greatly from the rich and varied experience and expertise of their independent panel members.

It is important that people with personal experience of adoption who may join a panel have the opportunity to consider how they may feel when drawing on their own experience in reading panel papers and in panel discussion.

Vice-Chair

Regulation 4(i)(b) requires the agency to appoint one or two people from the central list to be Vice-chairs. Guidance 1.29 confirms that there is no requirement for the Vice-chair to be independent of the agency 'though this would be preferable where feasible'.

Agency adviser to the panel

Regulation 8 requires that:

(1) *The adoption agency must appoint a senior member of staff, or where local authorities agree to constitute joint adoption panels as necessary, appoint a senior member of staff of one of them (referred to in this regulation as the "agency adviser"):*
   (a) *to assist the agency with the maintenance of the central list and the constitution of adoption panels;*
   (b) *to be responsible for the induction and training of persons in the central list;*
   (c) *to be responsible for liaison between the agency and the adoption panel, monitoring the performance of persons in the central list and members of the adoption panel and the administration of adoption panels; and*

   (d) *to give such advice to an adoption panel as the panel may request in relation to any case or generally.*

(2) *The agency adviser must be a social worker and have at least five years' relevant post-qualifying experience and, in the opinion of the adoption agency, relevant management experience.*

Guidance 1.30 states that: 'The person appointed should be someone with experience as an adoption team leader or someone who has more senior management experience and who has experience of adoption'.

The adviser is not a panel member and 'cannot take part in the decision making process They should be able to contribute to panel meetings by raising issues and providing advice, for example, about the agency's procedures and practices' (Guidance 1.31).

Guidance adds the following:

- *The agency adviser should maintain an overview of the quality of the agency's reports to the panel and liaise with team managers to quality assure the child's permanence report, the prospective adopter's report and the adoption placement report. Where there are concerns about a report, the agency adviser and the panel Chair should consider whether it is adequate for submission to the panel.* (Guidance 1.32)

- *It is recommended that the agency adviser also update the panel on the general progress of the cases it has considered.* (Guidance 1.33)

- *Arrangements should be made by the agency adviser to the panel for the safe keeping of the minutes and the record.* (Guidance 1.47)

The annual review of the performance of all panel members apart from the Chair is to be carried out by the agency adviser and the Chair (Guidance 1.35). This important shared duty of the agency adviser is described in more detail in the later section in the chapter, *Review of panel members*.

Legal advice

It is not a requirement for the agency's legal adviser to be a panel member and in practice very few are.

Regulations state that the panel 'must obtain legal advice in relation to the case' when considering adoption as the plan for a child (AAR 18(2)(c)). However, when considering the suitability of adopters or a match for adoption, the panel may obtain legal advice as it considers necessary in relation to the case (AAR 26(2)(c) and AAR 32(2) (c)).

Guidance 2.65 states that: 'Advice to the panel may be given orally and in writing'. In practice, it can be extremely helpful if the legal adviser attends meetings of the panel in person to give advice on each case and to answer questions which may arise in panel discussion. Even if it is not possible for the legal adviser to attend every panel meeting, it is likely to be very helpful if he or she sees the papers on every case and is able to alert and inform the panel in writing about any legal issues. If legal queries are not raised by panel members until the panel meeting and the legal adviser is not present and has not given legal advice, this could result in the case being deferred for legal advice. If the usual legal adviser is not able to be present, it is helpful if a well-informed colleague can attend in his or her place.

Attendance of non-panel members at panel meetings

The agency adviser to the panel, the minute taker and, often, the legal adviser will be in attendance at each meeting.

Clearly the social worker and, if possible, their manager should attend to present their case. When adoption is being considered as the plan for a child, it can be helpful for the child's foster carer or residential worker to attend.

When the suitability of prospective adopters is being considered, 'Before making any recommendation, the adoption panel must invite the prospective adopters to attend a meeting of the panel' (AAR 26(4)). Guidance 3.57 states that: 'This invitation should be extended to the prospective adopter each time the panel meets to discuss their case'. Many agencies also invite prospective adopters to attend the panel which is considering their match with a particular child. Prospective adopters' attendance at panel in both these situations is discussed further in Chapters 4 and 5.

The prospective adopter may with to bring a support person with them to panel. This is discussed further in Chapter 4.

Some panels have also, on occasion, invited a birth parent or a child or young person to attend panel. This is discussed further in Chapter 3.

Guidance 2.65 states that: 'The panel may wish to call for advice from those with relevant knowledge such as the CAFCASS children's guardian if care proceedings are ongoing, or specialists in education or child and adolescent mental health'. The panel should certainly ask what the children's guardian's views are, if one is involved with a child. If the guardian were to attend, this would be only for the purpose of answering questions or updating information in reports. The Chair will need to make it clear at the outset that this is the limit of the guardian's role at panel. He or she is not there to play any part in reaching the recommendation.

NMS 23.13 requires that each person on the central list is given an opportunity to observe a panel meeting before they sit on a panel. It can be helpful for social workers who may, in future, be bringing cases to panel, to attend a panel meeting as an observer. This can also be a valuable training opportunity for doctors and lawyers. However, there should not normally be more than one observer at panel. Attendance should be agreed by the agency adviser to the panel, if necessary in consultation with the Chair. Observers should sign a confidentiality agreement.

It is helpful if there is a feedback questionnaire for non-panel members, particularly prospective adopters and presenting social workers, who attend panel. Information can be collated and reported back to panel to inform practice. The feedback can also contribute to the performance review of the Chair and other panel members.

Quorum

Regulation 6 specifies that: 'No business may be conducted by an adoption panel unless at least the following meet as a panel'. These are:

- the person appointed to chair the panel or one of the Vice-chairs;

- a social worker with at least three years' relevant post-qualifying experience;

- three other members or four if the panel is a joint one. If the Chair is not present and the Vice-chair who is chairing the meeting is not independent of the agency, at least one of these members must be an independent person.

All these members must, as required by Regulation 4, be drawn from people on the agency's central list.

Appointment of substitutes

Although all members sitting as an adoption panel must be drawn from the agency's central list, Guidance 1.27 states that: 'There is no limit to the number of people who may be included on the central list'. Guidance 1.41 states that, subject to a panel being quorate, 'it is for the agency to decide how many panel members should be present at each panel meeting'. There is more discussion of this in the section on membership – practice issues.

Recruitment

Recruitment of adoption panel members has traditionally been largely through approaches to individuals based on personal recommendations. While this can work well, it can also lead to panel members being drawn from a rather narrow group of people already known to the agency.

Another method which is successfully used is direct approaches to the three main adoption self-help groups: NORCAP, a national self-help organisation for adopted people; Natural Parents' Network (NPN) for birth parents; and Adoption UK for adoptive parents.

These organisations can be asked to suggest individuals or can be asked to put a request in their newsletters. The Post Adoption Centres have also put requests for panel members in their newsletters (see Appendix IV). Some agencies have also advertised successfully in the local or national press. An internal newsletter could also be used to advertise for social worker members. Before doing this, an agency needs to be clear about what the task required is (job specification) and also what particular skills and experience they are looking for in this member (person specification). Applicants can then be short-listed and interviewed against open and clear criteria.

Sample job descriptions and person specifications for central list and panel members and Chairs are included in the appendices.

When there is a need for new members on the central list, existing members could be involved in discussion about the particular skills and expertise which may be lacking and which a new member could provide.

Central list and panel membership agreement

Guidance 1.28 specifies that: 'Before including an individual on the central list, the agency should inform them in writing of their performance objectives...The individual members should sign an acceptance form to record their agreement to these objectives.' The objectives given are:

- participation in induction and training;

- safeguarding the confidentiality of records and information submitted to the panel.

Additional points which could be included are:

- commitment to attend panel meetings as agreed with the agency;

- commitment to declare an interest and inform the Chair should a panel member have knowledge, in either a personal or professional capacity, of a case under consideration;

- commitment to anti-discriminatory practice and a preparedness to consider each case on its own merits;

- commitment to read the panel papers carefully and to come prepared to contribute to the panel discussion;

- arrival on time for panel meetings;

- willingness to consider attending an extra panel to deal with an urgent case;

- readiness to participate constructively in the annual review of their performance as a member;

- commitment to inform the agency at once if they have been charged, cautioned or convicted for any criminal offence or if any criminal proceedings are pending.

The adoption agency, for its part, should make a commitment to:

- provide induction training and written information to help prepare central list and panel members for the task, the written information to be updated as required. NMS 23.16 requires that 'each person on the central list has access to appropriate training and skills development and is kept abreast of relevant changes to legislation, regulations and guidance';

- arrange at least an annual training day for all central list and panel members;

- offer individual support and help, as far as practicable, should the member need or request this;

- undertake an annual review of the panel member's performance;

- send all the necessary information for each case at least five working days in advance of the date when the cases will be considered;

- assist members, if necessary, in the provision of a suitable, secure storage space for confidential panel papers while they are in the panel member's home;

- reimburse travel costs and consider the payment of a fee for reading panel papers and panel attendance;

- make available an opportunity for members to make representations or complaints to the agency;

- discuss informally any concerns about a panel member's behaviour or conduct in the panel and, if necessary, convene an additional review. If these concerns cannot be resolved, the agency will put in writing the reasons why it is ending the panel member's appointment.

There should be a central list and panel membership agreement that sets out these mutual commitments of the adoption panel member and the agency. It should be signed by the panel member and by a representative of the agency. This could be the agency adviser or the agency decision-maker.

Checks on central list and panel members

These apply to everyone on the agency's central list. They are listed in NMS 21.3. Every applicant must be interviewed and a record must be maintained of:

- identity checks;

- Criminal Records Bureau (CRB) disclosures;

- checks to confirm qualifications;

- at least two references, with written references verified by telephone;

- checks to confirm the right to work in the UK;

- where the person has lived outside the UK, further checks considered appropriate to supplement the CRB.

All social workers and others working with children are also required to have CRB checks. Although panel members will not usually have direct contact with children, they do receive comprehensive information on vulnerable children which could put children at risk if misused.

Prospective central list members will be asked to supply the names of two people who can give a reference as to their suitability as a panel member. There will also be discussion with the member about the professional and/or personal qualifications and experience which will inform their contribution to the panel. The agency will require evidence of qualifications and experience. Proof of identity, including a recent photograph, will be required.

Induction and training

NMS 23.13–16 specifies that:

- *The adoption agency provides each person on the central list with an opportunity of observing an adoption panel before they sit on an adoption panel.*

- *Each person on the central list is given induction training which is completed within 10 weeks of being included on the central list.*

- *Each person on the central list is given the opportunity of attending an annual joint training day with the agency's adoption staff.*

- *Each person on the central list has access to appropriate training and skills development and is kept abreast of relevant changes to legislation, regulation and guidance.*

It is important that central list and panel members are adequately prepared and trained for the job they do. Members should discuss their training needs at the annual review of their panel performance (see section on this) but should also raise issues and ask for information or help at any stage. The agency adviser and the panel Chair are the appropriate people to ask.

Members should be offered and should attend at least one day's training a year. Joint training with, for instance, members of the adoption team and with representatives from child care teams, on issues of common concern can be helpful. This can also be an opportunity for constructive feedback on how each group is perceived by the other.

It can also be helpful for members to have the opportunity for some training on working as a member of an adoption panel.

BAAF provides training in relation to adoption panel membership and for adoption and child care workers (see Appendix 4).

Review of central list and panel members

Central list and panel members must be given written information on what will be expected of them and also what they can expect from the agency, before they are appointed. This is detailed in the sections, *Central list and panel membership agreement* and *Induction and training*.

There is a requirement that there should be an annual review of each central list and panel member's performance. This will be conducted by the agency adviser to the panel and the panel Chair. The Chair's performance review will be conducted by the agency's decision-maker (Guidance 1.35 and 1.36). Suggested formats are included in the appendices.

Each member's performance will be reviewed against the written objectives agreed with them before their appointment. The review could provide a useful opportunity for a panel member to talk about any issues which may have inhibited his or her performance. These could include, for instance, a panel process which allows forceful or voluble panel members always to get in first with issues and questions or an agenda which is so tight that there is inadequate time for all panel members to contribute. It will also provide an opportunity for constructive feedback by the panel Chair and agency adviser on the panel member's contribution to panel meetings. It would be helpful if this could be evidenced by feedback from the other panel members and from presenting social workers and applicants who have attended panel. The need for further input or training could be agreed and arrangements made to provide this.

If, in that year, a person has never been invited to sit on a panel, they and the agency may decide that they should come off the list. It will clearly be difficult to review the performance of a member who has only sat on a panel a few times, or not at all. The member may wish to query how and by whom decisions are made to appoint people to a panel and the reasons why he or she him/herself has rarely or never been appointed.

The Chair's performance is reviewed by the agency's decision-maker, who may need to attend some panel meetings as an observer, to enable him or her to do the review. He or she should also seek views about the Chair's performance from other panel members, and from social workers and prospective adopters who attend panel (Guidance 1.35).

Brief feedback sheets for presenting social workers and prospective adopters who attend panel on the process as a whole, the role of the Chair and the contribution of any individual panel members are likely to be helpful. It might also be worth considering a form for panel members to use to make comments on the panel as a whole, on the Chair's contribution and on any other particular dynamics or issues.

Adoption panel fees

A local authority may pay to any member of an adoption panel constituted by it such fee as it may determine, being a fee of a reasonable amount (Regulation 4(4)).

Guidance 1.38 states that a voluntary adoption agency may also pay a fee to any member of its adoption panel.

Guidance 1.39 states that fees could either be for each panel attended or paid as an annual amount. Fees can cover preparation time as well as attendance at panel and expenses can also be paid for travel to and from panel meetings and related activities.

Many adoption agencies already pay fees to panel members. This enables them to recruit a wider range of panel members, not just those whose employer is prepared to donate their time or who can afford to give time on a voluntary basis. The Chair has a wider range of responsibilities than other panel members and will usually be paid a higher fee.

Tenure of office of members of the central list and adoption panel

There is no longer any requirement in regulations about tenure. However, there is nothing to prevent an agency from appointing people to its central list for a set period if it wishes. This would need to be set out clearly in the panel membership agreement, 'a signed document which sets out the mutual commitments of those individuals on the central list and the agency' – Guidance 1.3. Guidance 1.35 requires each panel member's performance to be reviewed annually and this could be an opportunity to extend an agreed period of appointment if both the agency and the member agree. The agency will need to balance the need for some consistency with the need for new recruits to the central list from time to time.

Resignation by central list and panel members

A person who is included in the central list may at any time ask to be removed from the central list by giving one month's notice in writing. (Regulation 3(2))

Any adoption panel member may resign at any time by giving one month's notice in writing to the adoption agency which appointed them. (Regulation 4(5))

Obviously, it is helpful if members can give more notice than this if possible, to enable a replacement member to be recruited.

Termination of appointment of central list and panel members

Where the adoption agency is of the opinion that a person included in the central list is unsuitable or unable to remain in the list the agency may remove that person's name from the list by giving them one month's notice in writing with reasons. (Regulation 3(3))

Where an adoption agency is of the opinion that any member of the adoption panel appointed by it is unsuitable or unable to continue as a panel member, it may terminate that member's appointment at any time by giving the member notice in writing with reasons. (Regulation 4(6))

Guidance 1.36 states that:

> *Where an agency identifies that the chair or an individual on the central list is not performing to the required standard, perhaps as part of the review process, it should ensure that this is discussed promptly with the individual with the aim of addressing any developmental needs through advice and training.*

Even if a review is not due, the agency adviser and the panel Chair might want to consider setting one up so that there can be a structured discussion with the member about their below standard performance. This might follow an informal discussion by the panel Chair and/or panel adviser with the member to try to resolve the problem. If it is the Chair whose performance is of concern, the agency decision-maker would need to be involved for further discussion and possibly for a formal review.

Adoption panel functions

The adoption panel has three key functions in relation to children and families. It must consider:

- *The case of every child referred to it by the adoption agency and make a recommendation to the agency as to whether the child should be placed for adoption.* (AAR 18(1))

It must also consider, and may give advice to the agency about:

> (a) *the arrangements which the agency proposes to make for allowing any person contact with the child; and*
> (b) *where the agency is a local authority, whether an application should be made by the authority for a placement order in respect of the child.* (AAR 18(3))

- *The case of the prospective adopter referred to it by the adoption agency and make a recommendation to the agency as to whether the prospective adopter is suitable to adopt a child.* (AAR 26(1))

It may also consider and give advice to the agency about the number of children the prospective adopter may be suitable to adopt, their age range, sex, likely needs and background (AAR 26(3)).

- *The proposed placement referred to it by the adoption agency and make a recommendation to the agency as to whether the child should be placed for adoption with that particular prospective adopter.* (AAR 32(1))

It must also consider and may give advice to the agency about:

> (a) *...the authority's proposal for the provision of adoption support services for the adoptive family;*
> (b) *the arrangements the adoption agency proposes to make for allowing any person contact with the child; and*
> (c) *whether the parental responsibility of any parent or guardian or the prospective adopter should be restricted and, if so, the extent of any such restriction.* (AAR 32(3))

These three functions are described in more detail in Chapters 3, 4, 5 and 6.

- Another key function of the panel is in relation to policies and procedures. The adoption agency must have written policy and procedural instructions governing the functioning of the agency and a panel, and such persons in the central list as the agency considers appropriate must be consulted about these (Regulation 7).

- Guidance 1.19 states that: 'Panels play an important quality assurance role providing objectivity and having the ability to challenge practice which is felt not to be in the interests of children or fall short of the Regulations or NMS. Panels are required to give regular feedback to the agency.'

This is described in more detail in Chapter 2.

Adoption and permanence panel

The consideration of the suitability of foster carers must be done by a panel which complies with the Fostering Services Regulations 2011. Fostering plans for children and matches for long-term fostering are not required to be considered by a panel and so there are no regulatory requirements. However, Guidance 1.23 states that:

> *Given the significance of long-term fostering, many agencies have established adoption and permanence panels, which combine knowledge*

and experience of adoption and fostering, and enable these two permanence options to be considered by one panel.

Some agencies consider permanence plans for children, including long-term fostering, at their adoption and permanence panel but approvals of carers and matches are considered by the fostering panel. However, as long-term fostering matches often develop out of a placement which was originally short-term, the plan for the child, the approval of the carer and the match are very interlinked and are probably best considered by one panel. This does mean, though, that the panel must comply with both fostering and adoption regulations. These are virtually the same. The only differences are that the social worker on a panel considering the approval or terms of approval of a foster carer should have experience of fostering work. Also, the Chair of a fostering panel does not have a casting vote, although the Chair of an adoption panel does. Chairs of adoption and permanence panels will need to keep this in mind.

Agencies will need to decide whether the adoption and permanence panel will also consider proposals for a looked after child to achieve permanence via a special guardianship order or a residence order. These considerations will often be in the form of a proposed match with an existing foster carer (who may or may not be a relative) who now wishes to apply for special guardianship or a residence order. As with long-term fostering, there is no requirement for a panel to consider these plans. However, the implications of a change of legal status are considerable for the child and for the carer. Special guardians can be assessed for a range of support services which are very similar to adoption support services. Adoption and permanence panel members are likely to have the knowledge and expertise to enable them to give valuable advice to the agency on these cases.

All foster carers must have their approval reviewed annually. Panels must see the first annual review report and may be asked to see others. (Approved adopters without a child in placement must also be reviewed annually, but there is no requirement to present a review to panel unless a termination of approval is planned. See Chapter 4 for a fuller discussion of this.)

There is further discussion in Chapter 3 about the panel's consideration of permanence options other than adoption.

Adoption reports

The key social work reports received by the panel are:

- the child's permanence report (CPR);
- the prospective adopter's report (PAR); and
- the adoption placement report (APR).

These are now required by regulation to be completed by workers who either have the necessary qualifications and experience or are supervised by someone who does. Social workers employed by the agency should have at least three years' post-qualifying experience in childcare social work, including direct experience of adoption work. This would include work with adoptive families or work in placing a child for adoption. If the social worker (or student) does not have this experience, they must be supervised by someone who does. An independent social worker, acting on behalf of the agency, must have the necessary experience and be supervised by someone who does (The Restriction on the Preparation of Adoption Reports Regulations (ARR) 2005).

Guidance 1.15 clarifies that it is not necessary for the supervised social worker to be under the direct line management of the supervising social worker.

Where reports are being completed by workers without the necessary experience, 'the draft report should be considered and discussed during supervision and signed off by a social worker with the necessary experience before the report is submitted to the adoption panel' (Guidance 1.16). It is likely to be helpful both for the inexperienced worker and for panel members if the supervising social worker can attend panel as well. The agency adviser to the panel could be asked to ensure that this happens.

Regulations specifically require the panel to consider all the information and reports passed to it by the agency. Where the panel considers that additional information is needed, it may ask for this and the agency 'must obtain, so far as is reasonably practicable, any other relevant information which may be required by the adoption panel and send that information to the panel' (AAR 17(3), 25(10), 31(5)).

Declaring an interest

Panel members who have had any involvement in a case to be considered, or who know any of the people involved, should declare an interest and should say whether they think this will prejudice their consideration of the case. If they do, they should not participate in that case, and it is probably best if they leave the room. If the panel member does not feel their knowledge will affect their consideration of the case, it will be the responsibility of the Chair, possibly with the help of the legal adviser, to make a final decision. It is important for panel members to alert the agency adviser or panel Chair as early as possible before the panel to avoid a possible problem over quoracy.

Reaching a recommendation

- Panel members must consider cases referred to them and make a recommendation to the agency.

- They must consider and take into account the reports sent to them.

- They may request the agency to obtain any further relevant information which they consider necessary.

- When considering the plan for a child they must obtain legal advice. When considering the suitability of adopters or a match they may do so.

- Panels can only make recommendations when they are quorate.

- Panels can make
  - a positive recommendation; or
  - a negative recommendation; or
  - defer making a recommendation until they have further specific information to enable them to do so.

- Although the Guidance makes no explicit reference to not making in principle recommendations, it makes clear that the decision-maker's decision must be based on a definite recommendation.

The panel Chair has a very important role. He or she should ensure that each panel member has an opportunity to ask questions or make comments on every issue. This may be facilitated by asking each member in turn for their questions and comments, starting with a different person each time. Each panel member should be asked whether he or she supports a proposed recommendation. Guidance 1.45 makes clear that: 'Where panel members have serious reservations, the panel Chair must ensure that these are recorded in the minutes and are attached to the panel's recommendations'. Guidance 1.45 further states that: 'If the panel cannot reach a consensus on its recommendation, after the chair and other members of the panel have voted, the panel chair has a second vote, i.e. the casting vote'. It will probably be helpful to both panel members and to the minute taker if the Chair summarises each recommendation made and the reasons for it, as well as any dissenting views, with reasons, during the meeting. This will ensure, as far as possible, that an accurate record is made.

Many cases are very complex, with risk factors as well as positive factors in relation to the issue for recommendation. It is important that there is rigorous consideration of the written information presented, and that relevant questions are asked of presenting social workers and of applicants, and their answers carefully considered. Many panels take time to formulate their issues and questions before presenting social workers and applicants are invited in to panel. Many panels also ask applicants and, less frequently, presenting social workers, to leave while they formulate their recommendation.

If panel members cannot reach a recommendation because important and relevant information is not available, they should defer making a recommendation. It should be made clear to the presenting social workers what additional information is needed, the realistic possibility of obtaining this should be discussed and a date should be set, if at all possible, for the case to come back to panel.

It is, however, important that deferring making a recommendation is not in fact an excuse for not coming to a conclusion when information is available. (There may be gaps but there may be clear reasons for these, e.g. information about a father whom a mother is unable to name or adamantly refuses to name.) All panel members should work hard to reach a view. Abstentions are not appropriate or helpful. No recommendation is likely to be risk free, and making a negative recommendation may result in a child drifting in the system, without a clear plan or without an adoptive family. However, it will sometimes be necessary, with the child's welfare always as the paramount consideration, to make a recommendation that a proposed plan, approval of a family or a match should not go ahead.

The decision-maker

Guidance 1.50 states that the decision-maker is a senior person within the adoption agency. VAAs may also appoint a trustee or director. This Guidance also states that 'there may be more than one decision-maker in an agency. The decision-maker may not delegate their authority to another person.' Agencies should therefore generally have at least two named and appropriately qualified decision-makers to ensure cover for any absence of one of them. Guidance 1.50 states that the decision-maker 'does not have direct management responsibility for the adoption panel'. NMS 23.17 requires, for the first time, that the decision-maker 'is a social worker with at least three years' post qualifying experience in child care social work and has knowledge and experience of permanency planning for children, adoption and child care law and practice'. In addition, where the adoption agency provides an intercountry adoption service, the decision-maker should have a good knowledge of intercountry legislation and practice.

Agency decision-making

The Regulations ensure that the panel has a separate identity from the agency, and is independent of it. The agency cannot delegate decision-making to the panel. However, it is required to refer certain matters to the panel (see section on *Adoption panel functions*) and to take its recommendations into consideration before making decisions on these matters.

Regulations make it clear that 'no member of the adoption panel shall take part in any decision made by the adoption agency' (AAR 19(2), AAR 27(2), AAR 33(2)).

Guidance makes it clear that, where the panel has provided the agency with advice, for example, about the range of approval for prospective adopters and about proposed adoption support services, contact arrangements and the exercise of parental responsibility in relation to a match, the agency

decision-maker may 'express a view on such advice'. The local authority must make a decision about adoption support services, contact arrangements and the exercise of parental responsibility. These decisions may be taken by the senior manager who is the agency decision-maker or by another manager (Guidance 2.68, 3.61 and 4.35).

It is important that, in drawing up its procedures, the agency ensures that a satisfactory means of communication is established between the agency decision-maker and the panel. If, for example, the decision-maker were repeatedly to refuse to accept the panel's recommendations, it would be necessary to have an arrangement whereby differing views could be explored. It may be helpful for the decision-maker to attend the panel as an observer occasionally (provided that he or she takes no part in proceedings or discussion). They may usefully also attend at least part of a training day with panel members. In complex cases, the decision-maker may want to clarify points with the Chair or agency adviser. The Chair and decision-maker must always be mindful, though, that the Chair cannot be involved in any way in the decision making.

Where the decision-maker is minded not to accept the panel's recommendation, he or she should discuss this with another senior person in the agency who is not a panel member. The outcome of this discussion must be recorded on the child's, the prospective adopter's, or both, case records (Guidance 1.56).

Administration

Good administrative arrangements are essential for the effective functioning of a panel. Responsibility for the administration of the panel is given by Regulation 8 to the agency adviser to the panel. He or she should ensure that sufficient administrative support is provided for the efficient performance of the tasks listed below. Any necessary training should be provided for the staff concerned.

The agency should, in consultation with panel members, determine the frequency and usual length of meetings and the number of cases to be considered at each. Many panels allocate about 45 minutes for consideration of a child's plan or the suitability of prospective adopters and perhaps an hour for consideration of a match.

There should also be a decision about whether or not forms need anonymising. Some agencies do this while others do not, and there are pros and cons of both practices.

Main administrative functions

Before panel meetings:

- Production of an annual schedule of meetings.
- Maintenance of a panel booking system.
- Notification to social workers of panel schedule and deadlines. Arrangement of accommodation and refreshments for meetings with, and if practicable, a private waiting area for, applicants and others attending the meeting.
- Preparation of agendas.
- Maintenance of records of panel members, their tenure, confidentiality bonds, etc.
- Working with the professional adviser, liaison with social workers and managers as required to ensure that the panel's requirements are met. This should include ensuring that social workers submit reports in good time, in the quantity required and in conformity with the panel's requirements.
- Responding to enquiries from social workers and foster carers about appearances before the panel, panel procedures and reporting requirements.
- Receiving of reports and bringing to the attention of the professional adviser any apparent gap.
- Ensuring that appropriate members and numbers are able to attend meetings to ensure a quorum.
- Liaison with the Chair about requests in relation to observers.
- Arranging for the copying and collating of papers and ensuring that they are sent out securely packaged to panel members.
- NMS 17.4 requires that 'all necessary information is provided to panel members at least five working days in advance of the panel meeting to enable full and proper consideration'.
- Ensuring that meeting and waiting rooms are prepared for the meeting, that name plates/badges are ready, that spare reports are available, that refreshments are ready, that recording equipment if used is functioning, etc.

At the meeting:

- Taking minutes, noting in particular, recommendations made and reasons given.
- Drawing to the attention of the Chair any matters requiring his or her attention.
- Collection of papers at end of meeting.

After the meeting:

- Drafting minutes, including recommendations made and reasons given.
- Submitting draft minutes to the Chair or professional adviser as appropriate for checking.
- Ensuring that the agency decision-maker receives the draft minutes and any other papers required for the decision to be made.
- Ensuring that applicants, foster carers and social workers are notified in writing of decisions.
- Providing the social worker with relevant minutes.
- Maintaining full records of panel business, including agenda, reports and minutes.
- Maintaining records for performance monitoring, government returns and the annual report.

Minutes

An adoption panel must make a written record of its proceedings, its recommendations and the reasons for its recommendations. (Regulation 6(2))

Guidance 1.44 specifies that:

The panel chair is responsible for ensuring the accuracy of the panel's recommendations, reasons and, following agreement with panel members, the minutes. The chair must also make sure that a person who is not a member of the panel fulfils the task of writing these documents.

Good minuting of panel meetings is essential. Guidance 1.45 states that:

It is important that the panel minutes carefully record the names of panel members attending the meeting, and the names and roles of any other people present at the meeting. The minutes must accurately reflect the discussion and cover the key issues rather than be a verbatim record of the meeting. Where panel members have serious reservations the panel chair must ensure that these are recorded in the minutes and attached to the panel's recommendation. The panel's minutes should clearly set out the reasons why the chair had to use the casting vote.

NMS 17.11 requires that the decision-maker makes a decision 'within seven working days of receipt of the recommendation and final set of panel minutes'.

The panel Chair will check draft minutes but a way will now need to be found to enable all panel members to check and agree draft minutes before they are sent to the decision-maker. Many agencies are emailing draft minutes to panel members within a day or two of the panel meeting and requesting speedy comments.

Guidance 1.52 further requires that the agency decision-maker must consider the minutes of the panel meeting, as well as all the reports submitted.

Minutes of the panel's consideration of adoption as the plan for the child and of a match should be put on the child's case record (AAR 12, 33). Minutes of the panel's consideration of the suitability of prospective adopters should be put on their case record (AAR 22).

BAAF has produced a useful pamphlet titled *A Guide to Writing Panel Minutes* (Pratt, 2011).

Disclosure of minutes

The agency has discretion to share minutes if it decides that this would be appropriate and helpful. However, the Adoption and Children Act 2002 (Consequential Amendments) Order 2005 amends the Data Protection (Miscellaneous Subject Access Exemptions) Order 2000 to provide for exemption from the right of access in respect of adoption records and reports.

Agencies should consider with their legal adviser whether or not to agree to disclosure. A principle of the Data Protection Act (DPA) which could be kept in mind when making this decision is whether the disclosure of information would identify another individual who has not consented to its disclosure. This could include, for example, information in the minutes about comments made by personal referees.

There is also an exemption in the DPA which extends to all social work records and which could be kept in mind. This provides that data need not be disclosed if doing so will be likely to prejudice the carrying out of social work by causing serious harm to the physical or mental health or condition of the data subject or another person. This means, for example, that an agency could refuse access to minutes to a birth parent if there was a serious risk that the anger this might induce in the parent might lead to an attack on a child, another parent or anyone else. Agencies should consider with their legal adviser whether or not to agree to disclosure.

Courts can order minutes to be disclosed as part of proceedings. A child's guardian in proceedings is entitled to see the child's case record, which will contain minutes of a panel which has considered a plan or match for the child.

Monitoring and review

It is recommended in Guidance 1.33 that the agency adviser should update the panel on the general progress of the cases it has considered. This could be in the form of three- or six-monthly reports on children and families considered since the last report, on children waiting for placement and also in placement but not yet adopted, and on waiting approved families.

It is also important that some time is set aside regularly for general issues to be raised by panel members or by the panel adviser. Some of these might need fuller discussion at subsequent panel training.

Guidance 1.19 states that: 'Panels play an important quality assurance role, providing objectivity and having the ability to challenge practice which is felt not to be in the interests of children or to fall short of the Regulations or NMS'.

NMS 17.2 requires that: '… adoption panels provide a quality assurance feedback to the agency every six months on the quality of reports being presented to the panel'. It will probably be helpful for the panel to note at the end of each panel, perhaps in a log kept by the Chair, any quality assurance issues which may have arisen. Some of these may need to be taken up with the agency straight away but they should also be noted for inclusion in the six-monthly report. NMS 22.8 specifies that the adoption panel which dealt with the case is informed of any subsequent allegations made against a prospective adopter or member of the prospective adopters' household and of the outcome of investigations into the allegation.

Review of panel work

It is good practice for the panel to produce a brief annual report. This could include information about membership, statistics, an account of activities and information on key issues of interest and concern. If such a report were to be circulated, it could help to integrate the work of the panel into the wider work of the agency.

Adoption inspection

Ofsted is the organisation responsible for inspecting adoption services every three years. (They also inspect fostering services annually.) An inspector will want to observe a panel meeting as part of the inspection, and will interview the Chair and possibly other panel members too. Panel members should ensure that they receive the conclusions of the inspectors, both about the panel and also about the adoption service in general.

Reference

Pratt J (2011) *Taking Minutes at Panel Meetings*, London: BAAF

2 Agency policy and practice issues

Making the adoption process work well

There is a section in the introduction to the Guidance – para 5, 'Making the adoption process work well' – which is included here, in summary.

The factors which experience and research have made clear can make the adoption process work well for the child, birth parents and adoptive parents are listed. They are, in summary:

- Actively promote adoption. A clear care planning process that always considers adoption as a possible permanence option.

- Encourage people to come forward to adopt.

- Avoid delay in the adoption process, including starting the family-finding process as soon as adoption becomes the plan following a statutory review.

- Take the fullest account of the views and wishes of the child.

- Place a child with a prospective adopter who can meet all, or most, of the child's identified needs.

- Provide an effective adoption support service.

- Collaborate effectively with the local authority's other social services and with voluntary adoption agencies.

- Develop and sustain constructive links between adoption and looked after children's teams and the courts.

- Have a practical and balanced understanding of the circumstances in which special guardianship may be more appropriate than adoption and how to manage the different processes and legal requirements.

Duties in relation to adoption

Local authorities have a legal duty under Section 3 of the Adoption and Children Act 2002 to:

> Maintain within their area a service designed to meet the needs, in relation to adoption, of –
>
> (a) children who may be adopted,

> (b) parents and guardians wishing to adopt a child,
>
> (c) adopted persons, their parents, natural parents and former guardians,
>
> and for that purpose to provide the requisite facilities.

Local authorities can arrange for registered adoption societies, or in some cases others, to provide services on their behalf. The services to be provided include arrangements for the provision of adoption support services and an intercountry adoption service.

The "welfare checklist" in relation to adoption

Section 1 of the Adoption and Children Act 2002 details an important "checklist" which applies:

> (1) ... whenever a court or adoption agency is coming to a decision relating to the adoption of a child.
>
> (2) The paramount consideration of the court or adoption agency must be the child's welfare, throughout his life.
>
> (3) The court or adoption agency must at all times bear in mind that, in general, any delay in coming to a decision is likely to prejudice the child's welfare.
>
> (4) The court or adoption agency must have regard to the following matters (among others) –
>
> (a) the child's ascertainable wishes and feelings regarding the decision (considered in the light of the child's age and understanding),
>
> (b) the child's particular needs,
>
> (c) the likely effect on the child (throughout his life) of having ceased to be a member of the original family and become an adopted person,
>
> (d) the child's age, sex, background and any of the child's characteristics which the court or agency considers relevant,
>
> (e) any harm (within the meaning of the

Children Act 1989 (c.41)) which the child has suffered or is at risk of suffering,

(f) the relationship which the child has with relatives, and with any other person in relation to whom the court or agency considers the relationship to be relevant, including –

(i) the likelihood of any such relationship continuing and the value to the child of its doing so,

(ii) the ability and willingness of any of the child's relatives, or of any such person, to provide the child with a secure environment in which the child can develop, and otherwise to meet the child's needs,

(iii) the wishes and feelings of any of the child's relatives, or of any such person, regarding the child.

(5) In placing the child for adoption, the adoption agency must give due consideration to the child's religious persuasion, racial origin and cultural and linguistic background.

(6) The court or adoption agency must always consider the whole range of powers available to it in the child's case (whether under this Act or the Children Act 1989); and the court must not make any order under this Act unless it considers that making the order would be better for the child than not doing so.

It is important for panel members to note that, for the purposes of this "checklist", references to "relationships" are not confined to legal relationships and references to a "relative", in relation to the child, include the child's mother and father.

It is crucial that this "checklist" is kept in mind by panel members in their consideration of every case.

Adoption is the plan for relatively few children. Recent statistics (DfE, 2011) indicate that just over four per cent of children looked after by English local authorities are placed for adoption, although there are wide variations between authorities. Roughly three-quarters of all children currently adopted in England and Wales have been looked after prior to adoption, most of the remaining quarter being adopted by step-parents or relatives – 3,050 looked

after children were adopted in England in the year ending 31 March 2011.

However, it is extremely important that good quality adoption services are available and that adoption is a well-recognised placement option for children. 'We know that in the vast majority of cases adoption works. Education and health outcomes are as good as for children growing up with their birth parents' (foreword to the Adoption Guidance).

Social workers and their managers, panel members and service users need good quality written information on adoption arrangements, policies and procedures and these need to be regularly reviewed.

This chapter describes some of the ways of achieving good policies and practice in adoption work and some of the issues that will need to be considered by agencies and panels. It is not an exhaustive list and panel members may well need to discuss other general issues with the agency.

Achieving good policies and practice in adoption work

Children's services plans

Adoption needs to be set in the general framework of the local authority's services for children. Local authorities are required to draw up and publish a plan of the services that they offer to children and their families and this should include details of their adoption services. It may be helpful for an extract from the local authority's plan to be included in the folder.

Child care policy

All children need the opportunity to experience permanence within their birth family or within a new family. Many agencies have a child care policy about planning for children's permanence needs within clear timescales to prevent drift. This might include the panel's role in reviewing children identified as needing a permanent new family but still waiting. If the agency has a written child care policy, this should be included in the folder.

Equal opportunities/diversity policy

If the agency has an equal opportunities or diversity policy, it will underpin the work of the panel. Panel members need to be aware of their individual attitudes and prejudices and also of the way that organisational processes can lead to unfair discrimination. However, it should be remembered that the overriding principle in adoption work is the duty to give paramount consideration to the welfare of the child. It will be useful for the equal opportunities policy to be included in the pocket on the back cover.

Child protection policy

The agency will have a child protection policy and procedures and it might be helpful for some information on these to be included in the pocket on the back cover.

Adoption panel policies and procedures

NMS 17.1 requires that:

The adoption agency implements clear written policies and procedures on the recruitment to and maintenance of the central list of persons considered by them to be suitable to be members of an adoption panel ('the central list') and constitution of the adoption panel.

Guidance 1.3 recommends that the following are included in the policy and procedures document for the adoption panel.

- Details of recruitment, induction, training and performance review of those individuals on the central list.

- A panel membership agreement. This is a signed document which sets out the mutual commitment of those individuals on the central list and the agency.

- Arrangements for informing the prospective adopter, the birth parents and, where appropriate, the child, of the panel's recommendations.

- Details of how a panel will monitor and report on its work to the agency and others.

- Arrangements and timescales for passing the panel's recommendations and minutes to the decision-maker.

It could also include information on how the agency will decide who to invite from the central list to sit on a particular panel. Who will make this decision? Will the agency aim to have a certain number of independent members at each panel meeting? Will it aim to have more members than the minimum quorum?

The panel's involvement in contributing to good practice

An adoption agency must, in consultation with such persons in the central list as the agency considers appropriate and...with the agency's medical adviser, prepare and implement written policy and procedural instructions governing the exercise of the functions of the agency and an adoption panel in relation to adoption and such instructions shall be kept under review and, where appropriate, revised by the agency. (Regulation 7)

The medical adviser must be consulted about arrangements for access to, and disclosure of, health information. Members should discuss with the Chair and the agency adviser how they can best be involved in this consultation. Some time at a training session could be set aside for comments on a draft set of policies and procedures. Central list members, as well as staff, should be given a copy of these policy and procedures documents.

In addition to this statutory involvement, panels have the potential to make an influential contribution to good practice. Panel members should recognise and feel confident about the important role that they can play. They should always question things which are not clear or which seem inappropriate and should ask for additional information if necessary. It is also important that some time is set aside regularly for general issues to be raised.

Central list and panel members should receive regular reports of the work of the adoption agency. This should include regular, perhaps three-monthly, brief reports on the circumstances of children and adoptive applicants awaiting placement and of children placed but not yet adopted. Unfortunately, not all placements will work out successfully. Members should be notified of any placements which have disrupted. Useful insights can be gained when panel members consider placements which have disrupted. It can be a good use of time if the panel considers the original reports as well as a report into what subsequently happened.

Specific issues which panel members will need to consider

The agency may have a formal policy agreed by committee or a clear view on some of the issues identified in this section. Central list members should be consulted as appropriate by the agency (see above) in the drawing up of written policies and procedures for adoption work and in reviewing these and should therefore be broadly in agreement with them. However, the panel is independent of the agency and panel members have a responsibility to consider each individual case carefully on its own merits.

There is no such thing as the "perfect" family or the "ideal" match. Panel members need to bear in mind that no recommendation which they make is free of risk. Strengths and limitations have to be identified and weighed and extra help and support specified to address gaps. Not making positive recommendations about the plan for a child, the approval of a family or the matching of a child may mean that a child waits longer in the care system and this could be a greater risk for them. However, panel members should also be clear that, with the child's welfare as their paramount consideration, it will sometimes be necessary to reach a view that a family or a match should not be recommended.

Family structures

- **Single parents.** Guidance 4.9 states that: 'Single prospective adopters of both genders can have much to offer an adopted child. They may be able to focus all their time on meeting a child's needs and have a good level of physical and emotional availability. Some children may find it easier to relate to just one parent or prefer not to relate closely to a mother or a father figure if there are negative associations from the past. Issues of emotional and financial support, health and future close relationships will need to be carefully explored with single prospective adopters.'

- **Child's position in the family.** It is most usual for children to enter their new family as the youngest child. However, placement as the eldest or middle child can be appropriate. It is important to know what position the child has held in the past to assess whether continuing or changing this may be the most appropriate for this particular child. The wishes and feelings of existing children in the family are also obviously crucial.

- **Age gaps between children.** Research (Sellick *et al*, 2004) shows that there is a higher risk of a placement not working out if a child is placed in a

family which has other children close to them in age. An age gap of at least two years is usually advisable.

- **Divorce or previously failed partnerships.** Panel members need to assess whether this is a pattern which could be repeated in the future. When there has been joint parenting experience with a previous partner, it is important to try and get the previous partner's view on how this worked. This issue is discussed in more detail in Chapter 4.

- **Unmarried partners can apply jointly for an adoption order.** For many years unmarried couples – lesbian, gay or heterosexual – have been assessed as adopters and have had children placed. However, until a few years ago, only one was able to apply for the adoption order.

- **A big age difference between two partners.** Practice has shown that people who are comfortable with difference can be very effective parents for children with special needs. However, please see also the paragraph on age in *Health and disability issues* later in this chapter.

References

The references required are detailed in the Adoption Agencies Regulations 2005. These include:

- written reports on interviews with three personal referees, not more than one of whom may be a relative;

- written information from the applicants' home local authority;

- a record of any criminal convictions from the police (see below).

In addition, some agencies also make enquiries of some or all of the following: previous partners, the probation service, National Society for the Prevention of Cruelty to Children (NSPCC), the education department, children's schools, the housing department, employers, the bank and/or building society. There is further information about checks and references in Chapter 4. Agency policy and procedure documents should make clear to panel members the range and number of checks and references which the agency requires, as this may be more than the statutory minimum.

Criminal background

AAR 23 provides that an adoption agency must obtain an enhanced criminal record certificate for the prospective adopter and any member of his/her household aged 18 or over.

The adoption agency may not consider a person suitable to adopt a child if he or any adult member of his household aged 18 or over –

(a) has been convicted of a specified offence committed at the age of 18 or over; or

(b) has been cautioned by a constable in respect of any such offence which, at the time the caution was given, he admitted.

The Rehabilitation of Offenders Act 1974 does not apply in the case of prospective adopters and therefore all criminal convictions should be listed on the police report. "Specified offences" are listed in Schedule 3 of the Adoption Agencies Regulations 2005. They are in the main offences of violence against children and sexual offences against children.

If between the time of approval and the time of placement of a child, or between placement and the making of an adoption order, a prospective adopter or an adult member of his or her household is convicted of or cautioned for a specified offence, the agency will be required to decide that the prospective adopter is no longer suitable and notify him or her accordingly. Where placement has already occurred, the agency must take immediate steps to remove the child unless the application to adopt has already been issued, in which case it will be a matter for the court. It would be appropriate for the panel to be informed if this occurs.

A criminal record of other offences need not rule out a prospective adopter. However, the nature of the offence, how long ago it was committed, and whether or not it was revealed by the applicant, will all have to be carefully considered. Panel members should know who the agency's liaison person with the police is and how sensitive information about criminal convictions is dealt with. They also need to know the details of any convictions and the applicant's permission for this should be obtained. It is not appropriate to obtain information about the circumstances of an offence only from the prospective adopter.

Health and disability issues

Medical conditions or disabilities should not necessarily rule out applicants. A health risk assessment should be made by the medical adviser and his or her advice will be extremely important. However, the panel recommendation should involve the views of all panel members.

The following health-related lifestyle factors should also be considered.

- **Smoking.** Does the agency have a policy in relation to applicants who smoke? There is evidence that smoking causes health problems for smokers and that passive smoking can damage the health of others, particularly young children. BAAF's Practice Note on smoking (BAAF, 2007) recommends that it is only exceptionally that children under five or those with respiratory problems are placed with carers who smoke.

  While stating that 'There is no legal reason why a child cannot be matched with a prospective adopter who smokes', Guidance 4.16 reiterates this: 'A local authority may have to restrict smokers as regards the age and type of child who may be placed with them, especially a child under five or who has a heart or respiratory problem or glue ear.'

- **Weight issues.** Obesity can cause health problems as can anorexia or other eating disorders. Is there evidence of unhealthy eating patterns or limited mobility, either of which could affect their parenting capacity? The medical adviser will advise on this.

- **Drinking.** Excessive alcohol consumption does lead to health problems. For many children in care, alcohol may have been associated with violence and physical abuse. The medical adviser will be able to advise panel members on the Department of Health recommended maximum alcohol consumption amounts.

- **Age.** General health and fitness obviously play an important role in determining an applicant's ability to parent children into adulthood. There is a greater health risk as people age. Agencies have a responsibility to maximise the chances of applicants remaining fit and well into their child's young adulthood. Guidance 4.10 states that: 'Where older children need adoptive parents, older and more experienced adopters could take on the care of these children if they enjoy sufficient health and vigour to meet the child's varied demands'. Guidance 4.11 cautions that: 'The age of the prospective adopter must also be considered in the light of the age gap between them and the child to be placed with them. Too large a gap may have an adverse effect upon the child.' Guidance 3.18 states that adoptive parents will need to 'have the health and vigour to meet the many and varied demands of children in their growing years and be there for them into adulthood'. Age is one consideration among many taken into account in assessing the suitability of prospective adopters.

Please also refer to the section on Health and Disability issues in Chapter 4, *Families offering placements*.

Lesbian and gay issues

The Adoption and Children Act 2002 allows unmarried couples, including those of the same sex, to adopt a child jointly.

There is a useful BAAF Good Practice Guide, *Recruiting, Assessing and Supporting Lesbian and Gay Carers and Adopters* (Mallon and Betts, 2005) which discusses and refutes some commonly-held myths.

Myth: The only acceptable home for a child is one with a mother and father who are married to each other.

Fact: Research shows that children thrive in many different types of family structure. In the UK, there are increasingly more diverse types of families.

Myth: Children need a mother and a father in order to have proper male and female role models.

Fact: Children get their role models from many people besides their parents. These include grandparents, aunts and uncles, teachers, friends neighbours and people in public life.

Myth: Gay men and lesbians do not have stable relationships and would not know how to be good parents.

Fact: Many lesbians and gay men are in stable, committed relationships and many are successfully involved in the parenting of children. All of the evidence shows that lesbians and gay men can and do make good parents.

Myth: Children raised by gay or lesbian parents are more likely to grow up gay themselves.

Fact: All of the available evidence demonstrates that the sexual orientation of parents has no impact on the sexual orientation of their children, and that children of lesbian and gay parents are no more likely than any other child to grow up to be gay. In fact, most lesbians and gay men have been raised by heterosexual parents. Of course, some children of lesbian and gay men will grow up to be gay, as will some children of heterosexual parents. There is some evidence that children of gay men and lesbians are more tolerant and open to difference.

Myth: Children raised by gay or lesbian parents will always be subjected to bullying and rejected by their peers.

Fact: Children make fun of other children for all kinds of reasons: for being short or tall, for being too thin or too fat, or for belonging to a different ethnic group or religion. Children can show remarkable resilience to this, especially if they have a stable, loving home environment and parents who can support them. Because of the homophobia that exists in society, some children will experience discrimination and negative comments for having lesbian or gay parents. This needs to be acknowledged and addressed. Adults who adopt or foster children need to have worked out strategies to support their children, who will already feel different or stigmatised because of not being with their birth parents.

Myth: Gay men are more likely to abuse children.

Fact: There is no connection between homosexuality and paedophilia. All of the legitimate scientific evidence supports this assertion. In a study examining cases involving sexual abuse of boys by men, 74 percent of the abusers were or had been in a heterosexual relationship with the boy's mother or another female relative (Jenny *et al*, 1994).

Discipline issues

The Fostering Services Regulations 2002 prohibit the use of corporal punishment by foster carers. Panel members need to be clear whether the agency has a policy on this in relation to adopters. What might the implications be of even a light smack for a child who has previously been physically abused? Does the agency have any policies about the types of discipline which are acceptable or unacceptable? Issues around discipline, including alternatives for managing difficult behaviour, should have been discussed with adopters and incorporated into the prospective adopter's report.

Matching policy in relation to culture, "race", religion and language

The Children Act 1989 requires that:

> *Before making any decision with respect to a child who they are looking after... a local authority shall give due consideration... to the child's religious persuasion, racial origin and cultural and linguistic background.* (Section 22)

The Adoption and Children Act 2002 section 1 also requires that: 'In placing the child for adoption, the adoption agency must give due consideration to the child's religious persuasion, racial origin and cultural and religious background'.

Guidance 3.16 states that: 'While children do tend to do better if adopted by a family who shares their ethnic origin or cultural group, these are just one of many considerations and must not be the primary consideration.' Guidance 4.6–4.8 gives additional advice. It cautions against 'placing the child's ethnicity above all else when looking for an adoptive family for the child'. It further states that 'a prospective adopter can be matched with a child with whom they do not share the same ethnicity, provided they can meet the child's other identified needs'. And that: 'The core issue is what qualities, experiences and attributes the prospective adopter can draw on and their level of understanding of the discrimination and racism the child may be confronted with when growing up.' And further: 'All families should help children placed with them to understand and appreciate their background and culture. Where the child and prospective adopter do not share the same background, the prospective adopter will need flexible and creative support to be given by their agency.' One of the main reasons for this guidance is concern that efforts to find adopters who can fully meet a child's identity needs is causing undue and harmful delay in placing children for adoption. Most agencies will have a policy in relation to meeting children's cultural and ethnic needs. This should be included in the pocket on the back cover.

Permanence

Mention has already been made, earlier in this chapter, of a general childcare policy which the agency may have. This should also be included in the pocket on the back cover. BAAF's position on children's need for permanence is included at the start of the following chapter.

Contact

Adoption with contact is a reality. The fact that a child may need ongoing contact of some sort should not rule out adoption as the plan. This is discussed further in Chapters 3 and 5.

Health and safety issues

Does the agency have any standard requirements with regard to health and safety issues in the applicant's home? If so, a copy of any such document should be attached. It can be helpful for children to have contact with pets. Does the agency have any health, safety and hygiene policies for children placed in relation to any animals, birds, reptiles or insects which applicants may keep in their home? Some agencies use questionnaires to gather information on pets and a copy of any such document should be attached. BAAF's Practice Note, *Placing children with dog-owning families* (BAAF, 2003) gives useful advice.

Financial matters

Details of the agency's policy and procedures in relation to financial support should be included in the pocket on the back cover. Panel members should have information on the agency's practice and procedures in relation to financial support for adopters, residence order allowances, special guardianship allowances, maintenance payments between placement for adoption and the adoption order, and settling-in grants and payments for equipment or house extensions. Panel members may wish to discuss these with the agency.

Family work patterns

Does the agency have a policy in relation to applicants working outside the home? It is probably most helpful to be fairly flexible about this while recognising, at the matching stage, that some children will need a parent at home with them full time for a considerable period. The support which the agency is able to offer, including the provision of financial support, may be crucial.

One adoptive parent is eligible for statutory adoption leave from work for a year. The first 39 weeks is paid, the subsequent period is unpaid. The other parent, in a couple, is eligible for two weeks "paternity" leave. Couples can choose who takes which leave, e.g. a male partner could take the adoption leave and a female partner the "paternity" leave.

Adoption support services

The package of adoption support services may well be a crucial factor when panel members are considering the viability of a placement. Panel members in local authorities need to be clear about what and how ongoing support is offered by the local authority, including help to access specialist health and education services when necessary. Panel members in voluntary adoption agencies also need to know about the adoption support services offered by their agency.

The placing local authority will be responsible for assessing adoption support needs for three years after the adoption order, after which this reverts to the area authority. Regular financial support and support in relation to contact remain the placing authority's responsibility.

Placements with family members or existing foster carers

All the above issues need equally careful consideration when birth family members or existing foster carers are being considered as permanent parents for a child. Guidance 4.13 recognises that local authorities are required to consider a placement with relatives if the child is unable to return to birth parents and that fostering or special guardianship may be the right plan, but states 'the appropriateness of adoption by a relative should not be automatically ruled out'. Guidance 4.14 states that there may be some circumstances where the security provided by the irrevocability of an adoption order and its lifelong effect would be best for the child and outweigh the potential drawbacks of the "skewing" of relationships. It references case

law to the effect that 'there is no presumption that a special guardianship order will be preferable to an adoption order if the placement is with a relative'. The benefits for the child of remaining within their birth family and/or of retaining an existing strong attachment need to be taken into account. However, these placements should not be viewed as a fait accompli. Guidance 3.24 states that: 'Foster carers who express an interest in adopting children in their care should be given advice about the fact that the adoption procedures apply in their case as in any other...Although foster carers have a legal right to institute their own adoption application, the local authority should encourage them to participate in the adoption agency process.'

Members of staff

Good practice suggests that applicants who are members of staff working for the adoption agency or for the Children and Families part of the Children's Services Department should apply to adopt to another agency. Consideration should be given to whether this requirement should also apply to all staff working for the Children's Services Department, in the interests of confidentiality and fairness. In the rare cases where the member of staff is interested in adopting a specific child or children looked after by their employing agency, the consideration of the matching could also be undertaken by another agency's panel.

Duration of approval

Regulations require an adoption agency to review, whenever it considers it necessary, and at least annually, the approval of prospective adopters who do not have a child placed or are not, in the case of an intercountry adopter, committed to proceeding with the adoption of a specific child. The agency is only required to refer the case to the panel if it considers the adopters are no longer suitable to adopt a child. In this situation, the same procedure must be followed as for the consideration of new prospective adopters.

Guidance 4.74 specifies that CRB checks should be renewed every two years. There is no statutory requirement about updating other checks and references but it would be good practice to do this every two years too. BAAF recommends that a medical update is obtained every two years. The agency should have clear written procedures on this.

The agency also needs to be clear about, and to make clear to the panel and to prospective adopters, what the procedure will be when a family has a disrupted placement before an adoption order is made. Good practice suggests that, if the family wishes to continue as approved adopters, the agency should formally review their case.

Representations and complaints

The Children Act 1989 complaints procedure which is set out in The Children Act Representations Procedure (England) Regulations 2006 requires local authorities to establish a procedure for considering representations, including complaints. These must be in relation to a specific child. They could include representations about cases which the panel had considered. For example, a foster carer might complain that, although adoption was the agency plan for a child in her care, she was still waiting two years later and nothing seemed to be happening. Agencies should normally inform panel members of representations about cases that the panel has considered.

Adoptive applicants can make representations, including complaints, to a local authority if the local authority has a power or duty to provide them with a service. Local authorities do have a general duty under Section 2 of the Adoption and Children Act 2002 to provide services for people wishing to adopt a child. Representations would have to be in relation to the service offered (or not offered) and would not be a method of appealing against an agency decision about suitability to adopt.

Representations and complaints can only be made to voluntary adoption agencies in relation to children for whom they are providing a service who are not looked after by a local authority. Adoptive applicants have the right to make representations to voluntary agencies under the Voluntary Adoption Agencies and the Adoption Agencies (Miscellaneous Amendments) Regulations 2003, Regulation 11. National Minimum Standards require that voluntary agencies should have procedures to enable users of their services to make representations, including complaints, about any aspect of the adoption service provided. It would be helpful to include a copy of these procedures in the pocket on the back cover.

When an agency decision-maker is proposing not to approve prospective adopters as suitable to adopt, they are entitled to an independent review of their case. This process is described in more detail in Chapter 4 in the section about the Independent Review Mechanism (IRM).

References

BAAF (2003) *Placing Children with Dog-owning Families*, Practice Note 42, London: BAAF

BAAF (2007) *Reducing the Risks of Environmental Tobacco Smoke for Looked After Children and their Carers*, Practice Note 51, London: BAAF

Department for Education and Skills (2005) *Children Looked After in England (including adoptions and care leavers): 2003–2004*, Norwich: The Stationery Office

Jenny C, Roesler TA and Poyer KL (1994) 'Are children at risk for sexual abuse by homosexuals?', *Pediatrics*, 94(1), pp 41–4

Mallon G and Betts B (2005) *Recruiting, Assessing and Supporting Lesbian and Gay Carers and Adopters*, London: BAAF

Sellick C, Thoburn J and Philpot T (2004) *What Works in Adoption and Foster Care?*, London: Barnardo's/BAAF

3 Considering adoption for a child

Introduction

Children normally experience permanence from the life-long commitment of their family network, which provides for them an experience of belonging, continuity and ongoing support.

Permanence is essential for children in order to provide them with a foundation from which to develop their identity, values and relationships throughout their childhood and into adulthood.

For most children permanence is achieved within their family of origin and every effort should, therefore, be made to sustain this situation. When separation cannot be avoided, the child should be restored to their birth parents or family as quickly as possible.

Where this is not in the child's best interests, an alternative family should be found which can provide continuous care and commitment to the child into adulthood. Such a family should be well equipped to meet the child's needs and should, if possible, reflect the child's ethnic, religious and cultural heritage, acknowledge and respect their family of origin and, where appropriate, maintain ongoing links and relationships which are responsive to changing needs.

This search needs to be balanced against the importance of minimising any delay in placing the child.

The routes to permanence are varied depending on the needs of the individual child. For some separated children, adoption will provide the best means of ensuring legal security together with lifelong commitments; for others, permanence might best be achieved through special guardianship, residence orders or foster care.

Whichever route to permanence is most appropriate, help and support to child and family, before and after placement, are essential.

The range of children considered by the panel

Some panels only consider children for whom adoption is the proposed plan. If long-term fostering is the plan, this will be considered elsewhere. However, an increasing number of agencies are setting up adoption and permanence panels to consider the cases of all children for whom a permanent new family is the plan, whether the proposal is to achieve this via adoption or via long-term fostering, or even via a residence order or special guardianship. Adoption panel members are well equipped to consider all the issues that are important when a permanent new family placement is the plan. The information gathered and the consideration of whether the proposed plan meets the child's needs should be of the same standard and given the same care and attention whichever route to permanence is proposed.

It is important that panel members are clear about whether or not they will be asked to consider children for whom long-term fostering (or other permanence options) is the plan. If they will not, they will need to be clear about how and by whom such decisions are made.

If the panel does consider children for whom long-term fostering or special guardianship is the plan, as well as children for whom adoption is the plan, it is important that panel members are clear in each case what the proposed plan is and what recommendations they are being asked to make. Many agencies with adoption and permanence panels have an upper age limit for the children for whom long-term fostering is considered. This is often around 12, but panel members need to be clear on this for their agency.

Panels may now be asked to consider whether a looked after child should be placed for adoption overseas. This is discussed in Chapter 6.

For information on the timing of referrals to the panel please see the flow chart, *Routes by which a child comes to the panel with a proposed adoption plan*, at the end of this chapter.

Panel functions

The adoption panel must consider:

> ...the case of every child referred to it by the adoption agency and make a recommendation to the agency as to whether the child should be placed for adoption. (AAR 18(1))

It must also consider and may give advice to the agency about:

> (a) the arrangements which the agency proposes to make for allowing any person contact with the child; and
>
> (b) where the agency is a local authority, whether an application should be made by the authority for a placement order in respect of the child. (AAR 18(3))

Timescales

Guidance 2.2 specifies that:

- *The child's need for a permanent home should be addressed and a permanence plan made at the* **four month** *review.*

- *The adoption panel should receive all necessary information from the agency within* **six weeks** *of the completion of the child's permanence report.*

- *The adoption panel's recommendation on whether the child should be placed for adoption should be made within* **two months** *of a review where adoption has been identified as the permanence plan.*

NMS 17.11 states that 'The decision-maker makes a considered decision that takes account of all the information available to them, including the recommendation of the adoption panel and, where applicable, the independent review panel, within **seven working days** of receipt of the recommendation and final set of panel minutes'.

The four-month review is the second review held four months after a child starts to be looked after by a local authority. However, the plan may not be adoption at this stage. It could be a plan for the child's permanent placement back at home with parent(s) or with extended family members.

Guidance is clear that, although these timescales should generally be adhered to, the paramount consideration must always be the welfare of the child. Where the agency is unable to comply with a timescale or decides not to, the reasons for this should be recorded on the child's case record.

Panel members should also ask the reasons for what may appear to be delay in getting a case to panel. While thorough work must be done with birth parents and extended family (see later section), this must be done within a timescale which meets the child's needs to be settled in their permanent family as soon as possible.

Information required

Regulations require that the panel is sent:

- the child's permanence report (CPR);

- the child's health report; and

- information relating to the health of the child's birth parents.

The medical adviser is required to prepare a summary of 'the state of the child's health, his health history and any need for health care which may arise in the future' (AAR 17(b)) for inclusion in the child's permanence report. It will probably be helpful if the medical adviser can also summarise relevant health information about the child's parents and siblings. The medical adviser will have the full health reports available at panel but these will not be circulated to each panel member unless so advised by the medical adviser. The panel may, however, request further information which could include some or all of the detailed medical reports.

Other specialist reports may be helpful if they contribute to a comprehensive picture of the child's needs. Case law *Re B* (2008) has given guidance on good practice in presenting expert reports to panel. It specifies that expert reports served in care proceedings that address the present and future needs of the child should be provided to panel members. Where reports are voluminous (as they often are), the sections setting out the experts' opinion, conclusions and/or recommendations should be provided. Any other summary should only be presented if it is in writing and has the written agreement of all parties to the care proceedings.

Case law has held that any views expressed by a child's guardian, if the case is in proceedings, should be conveyed to the panel.

The panel must consider all the reports presented to it and 'may request the agency to obtain any other relevant information which the panel considers necessary' (AAR 18).

The agency is required to meet such requests as far as it can.

Guidance 2.14 states that: 'It is vital that the preparation of the CPR and the meeting of the adoption panel dovetail with the court's timetable so that there is no delay for the child. In some cases, the referral of the case to the adoption panel may need to await the completion of further assessments ordered by the court. These may be of the parent's capacity to parent the child. Agreement should be obtained with those involved as to which assessments are to be completed before the case can be referred to the adoption panel.' Panel members should enquire whether there are outstanding assessments so that they can take a view on whether they need to defer making a recommendation or can consider the case without waiting for the result of a particular assessment.

If the panel decides to defer consideration of a case until it has fuller or more adequate information, a date should always be set, probably the next panel meeting, for the re-presentation of the case. The agency adviser to the panel has primary responsibility for "gatekeeping" and for ensuring the adequacy of the information sent to panel members.

Any concerns about the quality of information should be raised at the panel meeting and minuted. Either the Chair or the agency adviser should take the matter up with the child's social worker and his or her manager, or with senior managers.

Legal advice

The panel must obtain legal advice. This can be given verbally or in writing. It would be good practice for the legal adviser to be present at panel to answer any questions.

People attending the panel

The child's social worker will attend and it is important for his or her manager to attend too if at all possible. It can be very helpful if the child's current carer also attends. It is not usual for either the child or his or her birth parents to attend, although some agencies have offered this opportunity and

have found that it can be helpful. It is important that panel members are fully informed about the views of the child and his or her birth parents. They could be invited to write or send a recording to panel members or to the Chair, if they wish. The issue of a guardian in court proceedings wishing to attend is covered in Chapter 1, in the section titled *Attendance of non panel members*.

Welfare of children

The panel, like the agency, is bound by the duty set out in Section 1 of the Adoption and Children Act 2002. This is given in full in Chapter 2 and should be the overarching context in which the plan for a child is considered. Key points are that:

- the paramount concern should be the welfare of the child, throughout his or her life;

- the child should be involved and consulted at all stages in the adoption process and his or her wishes and feelings taken into account in a way which is sensitive to, and consistent with, his or her age and understanding.

The child's permanence report

The information to be included in this report is detailed in Schedule 1, parts 1 and 3, of the AAR, and in AAR 17. It must include the following.

Information about the child (Schedule 1 Part 1)

- Factual information about the child, e.g. date of birth, ethnicity, religion, legal status.

- Chronology of the child's care since birth.

- Description of personality and of social, emotional and behavioural development.

- Education issues including any special needs.

- Relationships with birth parents, siblings and others, including:
  - the likelihood of the relationship continuing and the value to the child of it doing so, and
  - the ability and willingness of parents or others to meet the child's needs.

- Current contact arrangements with parents, relatives and others.

- Interests, likes and dislikes.

Information on the child's family and others (Schedule 1 part 3)

- Current factual information on the child's parents, siblings and other relatives.

- A family tree, including information about grandparents, aunts and uncles and parents.

- Clarification of who the father is and whether he has parental responsibility.

- Chronology of each parent since birth, including educational and employment history.

- Parents' experience of being parented.

- Their relationship, past and present.

- Details of wider family, their role and importance.

- Their parenting capacity, particularly their ability and willingness to parent the child.

Additional information (AAR 17)

- A health summary by the medical adviser on the child's health, health history and anticipated future health needs.

- The child's wishes and feelings about:
  - adoption
  - religious and cultural upbringing
  - contact with birth family and others

- Wishes and feelings of parents about:
  - the child
  - the plan, including religious and cultural upbringing
  - future contact

- Agency's views on and plans for contact.

- Assessment of the child's emotional and behavioural development.

- Assessment of parenting capacity of parents.

- Chronology of decision and actions taken by the agency.

- An analysis of options for future care and 'why placement for adoption is considered the preferred option' (AAR 17(1)).

  BAAF has published Form CPR, a template which enables agencies to be compliant with the regulations in relation to the child's permanence report. It is up to agencies to decide which format to use.

Issues to consider

The following list indicates some of the issues which panel members will need to consider when reading reports on children and formulating questions for the child's workers and carers. It is not intended to be exhaustive and other issues may well need to be addressed in individual cases.

The child's birth family

Panel members will need to be clear about how and why the child came to the attention of children's services and why the plan is now adoption. They will need to know what work has been done with birth family members and whether anything more could be done to help the child's birth family provide a home for him or her. The agency has a duty to counsel birth parents in relation to the adoption plan. NMS 12.3 requires them to have access to a support worker independent of the child's social worker from the time adoption is identified as the plan for the child. Panel members must be clear that all other possible options for the child to remain with his or her birth parents or extended family or other people significant to the child have been fully explored. They need to be clear what the views of the child's birth parents and other family members are about the adoption plan.

In particular, panel members should check that the child's father, whether or not he is married to the mother, has been contacted and his wishes and feelings ascertained. This should be done unless there are clear reasons against it. There is useful guidance and case law on this in Guidance 2.35 – 2.43. The paramount consideration, as always, is the welfare of the child. The birth mother's wishes are a factor and, crucially, in the case of a father without parental responsibility, the role he has played in the child's life and in life with the mother and any other siblings. Each situation must be considered carefully on its own merits and is a matter for the agency's or court's discretion.

Panel members should check whether birth parents have seen the permanence report. Guidance 2.61 states that birth family members should be asked to check the accuracy of factual information. In addition the birth parents 'should be shown those parts of the report which set out their views and wishes, and given the opportunity, if they so wish, to express these in their own words'. The Guidance continues: 'Where the child is old enough, they should also be encouraged to confirm that their views have been accurately stated'.

(See also sections on contact issues below.)

What does the child understand and feel about what has happened and what is planned?

The child's wishes and feelings must be ascertained and given due consideration having regard to his or her age and understanding when making any decision about adoption for him or her (section 1 of the Adoption and Children Act 2002 quoted in full in Chapter 2).

The child will have experienced separations and loss and may well be confused, angry, sad and bewildered. It will be important for panel members to try and assess the child's understanding of what has happened and why, and of what is planned for them. Who is doing direct work with the child and how is this progressing? It can be very helpful for the panel to hear first hand from the child's foster carer or residential social worker, as well as from their social worker. Is there further work that needs to be done before the child can be placed in a new family?

Guidance 2.51 states that: 'The agency may also provide the child with a copy of the [permanence] report, or parts of the report, where he or she is of sufficient age and understanding and the agency considers it appropriate'.

Identity issues

Is there clear written information on the child's cultural, racial, religious and linguistic heritage? It will be important for panel members to have as much information as possible about the child's birth father as well as their mother. What sense does the child have of his or her heritage and identity? Is the child living with carers who reflect the child's identity? Panel members should consider whether there is any work which relates to identity that needs to be done before the child can be placed in a new family and should find out what the plan for this is.

Attachment issues

The child's early attachment experience will be a crucial factor in his or her ability to grow into a secure, self-confident person able to make new attachments. Poor early experience of attachments which may have been inconsistent, abusive, neglectful or constantly changing will have a profound effect on the child and will have considerable long-term implications for him or her and for the new parents. Panel members should ensure that they have full information on the child's attachment experience from birth. It will be important to have information about the quality of the child's attachment to the current carers and other significant people. Panel members should ascertain what help and support will be given to the child, to the carers and to the new family in the process of building, maintaining and transferring attachments.

Abuse and neglect issues

Many, if not most, of the children whose cases come before the panel will have experienced abuse, either physical or sexual or both, and neglect, either physical or emotional, or all of these. It will be important for panel members to be clear about the known facts about what has happened to the child. They also need to be aware that much more may have happened than is currently known. It is important to consider the following: What impact do the child's experiences of abuse and neglect have on their functioning and behaviour? What help is being given to the child and their current carers to deal with these issues? What are the long-term implications for a new family and what future help and support are the child and their new parents going to need?

Behavioural issues

Panel members will need up-to-date information on the child's behaviour in different settings, for example, in the foster home and at school. How does the child relate to other children and to adults? Information on how the child reacts to change will be important. Panel members should bear in mind that foster carers are used to looking after children with challenging behaviour who then move on and that children sometimes "contain" their feelings and behaviour until they are somewhere secure. There is thus a possibility that the child's problems may be underestimated. What help are the child and the carers currently receiving to manage any challenging behaviour and what is likely to be needed in the future?

Health and disability issues

The majority of children whose cases come to panel are already being looked after by the local authority and may have been known to the medical adviser for some years. Children for whom adoption is the plan are required by AAR 15 to have a comprehensive medical assessment and examination covering physical, developmental and emotional issues. The medical adviser may advise that this is not necessary if, for instance, there is already a report which includes the required information (Guidance 2.50 and 2.51). It is helpful if the medical adviser is also the doctor involved in the health assessment of children who are to be placed for adoption. This is often not possible but when it is, the medical adviser will usually be the only panel member who has met the child.

As well as evaluating the child's physical and emotional health and development, the medical adviser will also gather as much information as possible about the health of his or her birth parents and siblings and about any genetic implications for the child. He or she will also arrange for any further tests or examinations or treatment which may be necessary for the child. A summary by the medical adviser of the health history and state of health of the child and his or her parents, with comments on the implications for adoption and on how any special health needs of the child might be met, will be included in the child's permanence report, while the medical adviser retains the fuller reports. It is important that the medical adviser is available to interpret and advise on any health issues. If the child has a need arising from a particular health problem, condition or disability which affects day-to-day living, it will be important for panel members to have information from the current carers about this.

Education issues

Panel members will need written information on the child's current functioning and likely future needs. This should be covered in the child's permanence report supplemented as necessary by a school report, an educational psychologist's report, and the current carer's observations.

Needs of siblings

The panel should consider each child as an individual in his or her own right with needs as described above, as well as a member of a sibling group.

Panel members should also raise the following issues:

- Who are the child's siblings?

- Why are siblings being placed separately if this is the proposed plan?

- Why are siblings, who may have very great and perhaps conflicting needs, being placed together if this is the proposed plan? It will be important to check whether siblings have been involved together in abusive situations and, if they have, whether they can break the abusive ways of relating that they have learned, as long as they remain together. Has appropriate work been undertaken with these children to facilitate change?

- How do the children get on with each other? The observations of their carers will be important and the agency may also have completed the sibling relationship checklist in *Together or Apart? Assessing brothers and sisters for permanent placement* (Lord and Borthwick, 2008).

- What are the wishes and feelings of the children themselves about being placed together or separately?

- If the children are currently living apart but the plan is for placement together, what is being done to maintain or build a relationship between them?

- If the plan is for separate placements for siblings, what sort of contact between them is planned?

- What additional financial support may be available for a new family taking on a sibling group? Large sibling groups of five or six children can be found adoptive families but a package of financial support is often a vital factor in the viability of these placements.

Regular financial support can be paid to enable a sibling group to be placed together and to enable a child to join his or her siblings in an adoptive family (ASR 8(2)(c)).

Guidance 4.12 states that: 'Siblings should be adopted by the same prospective adopter unless there is good reason why they should not be. Where an agency is making a placement decision on two or more children from the same family it should be based on a comprehensive assessment of the quality of the children's relationship, their individual needs and the likely capacity of the prospective adopter to meet the needs of the siblings being placed together.'

Permanence options

The permanence report must contain an analysis of the options for the future care of the child which have been considered by the agency and why placement for adoption is considered the preferred option AAR 17(1)(i).

- **Adoption** offers legal security to a child, giving their adoptive parent exclusive and irrevocable parental responsibility. The legal parent–child relationship is for life. However, some form of contact with the child's birth family is quite common. This may be an annual exchange of letters via the adoption agency or it may be face-to-face contact, possibly with siblings or grandparents or sometimes with birth parents. Adoptive families have the right to be assessed for a range of support services at any time until the child is 18, and a range of services, including financial support, is often in place from the time of the child's placement.

Other permanence options are:

- **Returning the child** to his or her parent(s) with support where necessary. This is the preferred option if it can offer good enough and safe care to the child. The reasons why this is not possible must be clearly given and evidenced in the permanence report.

- **Placement with a relative.** This should have been explored, preferably using a Family Group Conference to mobilise all family members and to involve them in plans for the child's future. Relatives on both the mother's and the father's side of the family should be described in the report as well as their views and capacity to care for the child. A placement with relatives could be secured via adoption, special guardianship, a residence order, long-term fostering or possibly with no order.

- **Remaining with existing foster carers.** This will provide continuity for the child and may well be what a child wants. Permanence could be achieved via adoption, special guardianship, long-term fostering or a residence order. Guidance 3.14 states that foster carers who express an interest in adopting children in their care should be given

advice about the procedures that will apply in their case. The benefits of continuity and of maintaining a good attachment and avoiding a move for a child do need to be weighed against other factors. The placement may be transracial, the carers may be much older than usual, they may be offering long-term fostering when the child needs legal permanence. These may well be compromises worth making, but this does need to be given careful consideration.

- **Long-term fostering.** Research indicates that this can provide a sense of permanence for some children and young people. Their birth parents retain parental responsibility and may remain in quite frequent contact. Foster carers can work in partnership with the local authority and receive a fostering allowance which is not means tested and may include a fee. The child will receive ring-fenced services available to looked after children, including leaving care provision. However, he or she will remain a "foster child", subject to statutory visits and reviews, which may be felt to be stigmatising by some children. The foster carers will not have parental responsibility, which is shared instead by the local authority and birth parents. The local authority could decide to move the child and the parents could decide to apply to court for revocation of a care order. So, legally the placement is not secure, although in practice, with co-operation between all the parties, it may feel so to the child.

- **Residence order.** Foster carers or relatives could apply to court and be granted a residence order. This can last until the child is 18, gives the carer parental responsibility but does not remove this from the birth parent(s). The child ceases to be looked after by the local authority, although the authority has discretion to pay a residence order allowance to the carers. Support can be offered by the local authority although there is no statutory requirement to do so, other than to the child as " a child in need".

- **Special guardianship.** This is an order introduced under the Adoption and Children Act 2002. Guidance on special guardianship describes the need for 'an alternative legal status for children that offered greater security than long-term fostering but without the absolute legal severance that stems from an adoption order'. This was based on research indicating that 'children generally preferred the sense of security that adoption gives them over long-term foster placements. However, research indicated that there was a significant group of children, mainly older, who did not wish to make an absolute legal break with their birth family that is associated with adoption.'

Special guardianship does not remove parental responsibility from birth parents but it enables the special guardian to exercise their parental responsibility to the exclusion of all others, other than in a few very specific situations. The child is no longer looked after. However, if they were previously looked after, they and their special guardian(s) must, if they request, be assessed for support services, including financial support. These services equate almost exactly with adoption support services, but also include access for the formerly looked after child to leaving care provisions. Special guardianship orders are made by a court and can be made in favour of one or more people, who do not need to be married. Orders can be revoked, but the thresholds for applying are high, and so they offer legal security, even if it falls short of that offered by adoption.

- **Residential care** is a possible option for a child with very significant disabilities or other special needs for whom no family can be found, or for whom family care is not feasible or appropriate. This may only become the plan when the agency has failed to find a family for the child or when several family placements have disrupted. For a small group of children and young people, it may offer the best form of care and the one most acceptable to them.

Practice considerations in relation to permanence options

Guidance on adoption and permanence panels in 1.22–1.24 acknowledges that fostering plans for children are not required by regulations to be considered by a panel. It goes on to say:

> However, given the significance of long-term fostering many agencies have established adoption and permanence panels, which combine knowledge and experience of adoption and fostering and enable these two permanence options to be considered by one panel.

> Although it may be clear that a child needs permanence in a new family, the options for achieving this need careful scrutiny and for some

children it may be very difficult to find a new permanent family. An adoption and permanence panel would be well placed to consider adoption or long-term foster care. It may recommend that the child should be placed for adoption, or, if it considers that adoption would not best meet the child's needs, it could advise that the child should be placed into long-term foster care. This reduces the time needed to identify the type of placement that is most likely to meet the child's needs by avoiding consideration of adoption or fostering at separate panel meetings.

Some children will be referred to an adoption and permanence panel for whom the plan is adoption and others will be referred for whom the plan is long-term fostering or possibly special guardianship or a residence order. In each case, panel members should keep in mind the strengths and limitations of all the permanence options described in the preceding section.

Clearly a consideration of the child returning to one or both birth parents must come first. This should be followed by a consideration of extended family members. This option and that of remaining with existing foster carers could be via adoption, special guardianship, a residence order or long-term fostering.

All these permanence options need to be kept in mind before a permanence recommendation is made. The advantage of an adoption and permanence panel is that it is not limited to only making adoption recommendations. Even if an adoption recommendation is made, that panel can acknowledge that, for some children, it may be extremely difficult to find an adoptive family. Case law *Re P* 2008 clarifies that dual planning for adoption and long-term fostering is possible with a concurrent search for adoptive and fostering placements. The panel will need detailed information on adoption family finding to ensure that enough efforts have been made to achieve an adoptive placement.

Contact issues

The panel must consider and may give advice about the 'arrangements which the agency proposes to make for allowing any person contact with the child' (AAR 18(3)). The "welfare checklist" in section 1 of the Adoption and Children Act 2002 (see

Chapter 2), which must be considered in relation to every case, includes a duty to consider the child's relationship with relatives and others. The agency's views on contact and plans for this must be included in the child's permanence report and this must include both the child's wishes and feelings and those of his or her parents and other relatives.

Panel members need to understand and to check that birth parents understand that, once a local authority is authorised to place a child for adoption, either because it has a placement order or because parents have given formal consent, there is no presumption for or against contact. Any previous contact order ceases to have effect as does the 1989 Children Act duty to promote contact. The individual child's welfare becomes the paramount consideration in any consideration of contact arrangements.

A plan for face-to-face contact with parents, birth relatives and other people significant to the child need not rule out adoption. However, it will be important to be clear about the purpose of future contact and the value to the child. Panel members should ask about the type, frequency and quality of current contact and who is involved.

- What are the plans for contact after placement?

- Do the birth family members agree with the plans?

- What are the child's wishes and feelings about contact after adoption?

- What help and support do the agency plan to offer to facilitate contact arrangements after adoption?

Giving advice on whether a placement order should be applied for

The panel must consider this and may give advice to the agency.

In cases where parents do not agree with the adoption plan, the local authority has no choice but to apply for a placement order. It cannot place the child for adoption until a court has made a placement order except for children with no parent or guardian. The grounds for the making of a care order must be met, or there must already be a care order, before a placement order can be made. It suspends a care order, but this will be reinstated should the placement order be revoked before an adoption order is made. The court can make a

placement order without first making a care order if the grounds are met. However, it may be best for the local authority to make concurrent care order and placement order applications, so that a care order could be in place should the placement order be revoked.

Case law *Re T* 2008 clarifies that a placement order should usually be made at the same time as a care order when adoption is the plan, even if it may prove difficult to find suitable adopters.

If there is already a care order in place and the parents consent to adoption, the local authority may either apply for a placement order or it may place for adoption with consent. This consent must be witnessed by a CAFCASS officer. Placing with consent will avoid the work and possible delay of a court hearing. However, there is the risk that the parents could change their minds. Should they do this before the child is placed, the placement would need to be delayed until a court had made a placement order. Should they do this after placement but before an application for an adoption order, the local authority could apply for a placement order, which would prevent the child's removal. A possible advantage of applying for a placement order before placement is that it would give relatives the chance to be heard and to give their views on the adoption plan.

A placement order may be revoked on the application of the local authority or the child. Anyone else may only apply with the leave of the court and only if the child has not yet been placed for adoption. Unless revoked, a placement order will continue in force until the child is adopted, reaches 18, marries or forms a civil partnership.

Guidance 2.67 covers these issues.

Conditional or "in principle" recommendations

Although the Guidance makes no explicit reference to not making "in principle" recommendations, it makes clear that the decision-maker's decision must be based on a definite recommendation.

Many, if not most, cases of plans for a child are presented to panel during care proceedings. The agency must have a clear care plan for adoption before it refers the case to the panel for recommendation that the child should be placed for adoption. This cannot be conditional on the outcome of any assessments of birth parents or extended family members, or for any other reason.

Any advice which the panel gives about a twin-track or parallel plan and about the likelihood of it recommending adoption at some point has no clear status. The case will need to come back to panel at the point at which the agency is clear that it considers adoption to be the best plan for the child. The panel will not be bound by any previous advice it may have given. It is the local authority which needs to have a clear adoption care plan. The guardian may not agree with this (and his or her view must be made known to the panel). The court may also not subsequently endorse the plan by declining to make a care order and/or a placement order. However, the panel must make its recommendation based on a referral to it by the agency with a clear request for adoption to be recommended as the best plan.

Where, in the course of the court proceedings, new information comes to light which might affect the views of the panel as to the appropriateness of adoption, the case may need to be referred back to panel.

Minutes

Guidance 2.64 gives additional advice on minutes. They should record all the documentation considered by the panel so that it is clear which assessment reports were considered. Also, 'the social workers who attend the panel meeting to present the child's case should be invited to approve the record of the note of the questions asked of and answers given by them during the panel'. It may be helpful for the panel Chair to confirm with both the worker and the minute taker, at the meeting, exactly what has been said and recorded on particularly complex points.

What next?

A panel recommends whether a child should be placed for adoption and the agency then makes a decision about this. The panel may then not hear about the child again until a matching with prospective adopters is presented.

Panel members could ask at the meeting at which they make their recommendation about what actual steps will be taken to identify a family, and whether referral to other agencies for a possible

interagency placement is planned to minimise delay. They should also request regular, perhaps three- or six-monthly reports on waiting children and on waiting families. Guidance 1.55 specifies that 'the agency adviser should also update the panel on the general progress of cases it has considered. This is particularly important where the panel's recommendation or advice was not accepted.'

A flow chart, *Process for identifying a family after a decision that a child should be placed for adoption*, is reproduced at the end of Chapter 5.

Occasionally, circumstances in the birth family change significantly and there seems a real possibility that a child could live with a family member, even though an adoption plan has been made. In other cases, permanent fostering may come to seem a more realistic option for a child than adoption. Good practice requires that any proposed change of plan is brought back to panel at an early stage for consideration and, if appropriate, for a recommendation to rescind the adoption plan.

References

Lord J and Borthwick S (2nd edn) (2008) *Together or Apart? Assessing brothers and sisters for permanent placement*, London: BAAF

Sellick C, Thoburn J and Philpot T (2004) *What Works in Adoption and Foster Care?*, London: Barnardo's/BAAF

Further reading

Lowe N and Murch M (2002) *The Plan for the Child: Adoption or long-term fostering*, London: BAAF

Neil E and Howe D (eds) (2004) *Contact in Adoption and Permanent Foster Care: Research, theory and practice*, London: BAAF

Ryan T and Walker R (2007) *Life Story Work*, London: BAAF

Schofield G, Beek M and Sargent K with Thoburn J (2000) *Growing up in Foster Care*, London: BAAF

Schofield G and Beek M (2008) *Achieving Permanence in Foster Care*, London: BAAF

Schofield G and Ward E with Warman A, Simmonds J and Butler J (2008) *Permanence in Foster Care: A study of care planning and practice in England and Wales*, London: BAAF

Routes by which a child comes to panel with a proposed adoption plan

4 Families offering placements

Introduction

The primary purpose of recruiting and approving any family is to meet the needs of children. NMS require the agency 'to implement an effective strategy to recruit and assess prospective adopters who can meet most of the needs of those children for whom adoption is the plan' (NMS 10.1). No particular type of family should be excluded from consideration since the structure of a family does not indicate what the adults' capacity as parents may be. Legislation does not exclude any family structure as inappropriate for children's upbringing. Consideration of parenting abilities does, however, require evidence of the prospective parents' values and attitudes, life experiences, commitment, and flexibility in responding appropriately to individual children. Experience has shown that single people, older couples who already have children, gay men and lesbians, people who have remarried, childless couples, and people with disabilities can all have a great deal to offer specific children.

It is important for panels to remember that the great majority of children joining new permanent families will have undergone experiences quite unlike those of most other children in the community. Their new parents will therefore need to have been properly informed and prepared and will need support afterwards.

Guidance 3.10 specifies that: 'The agency should develop a plan for recruiting and preparing sufficient prospective adopters who can meet the needs of children waiting for adoption...The plan should help the agency focus its recruitment on groups of prospective adopters and to prioritise applications according to the needs of children waiting for adoption.'

Issues for families seeking intercountry adoption are covered in Chapter 6 since there are issues particular to intercountry adoption over and above those relating to domestic adoption which need to be carefully considered.

It may be helpful to refer to the flow chart, *Families offering placements*, at the end of this chapter.

Function of the panel

The adoption panel must consider the case of the prospective adopter referred to it by the adoption agency and make a recommendation to the agency as to whether the prospective adopter is suitable to adopt a child. (AAR 26(1))

Where the adoption panel makes a recommendation that the prospective adopter is suitable to adopt a child, the panel may consider and give advice to the agency about the number of children the prospective adopter may be suitable to adopt, their age range, sex, likely needs and backgrounds. (AAR 26(3))

The range of families available

Families being considered at the panel will fall into one of three different categories:

- relatives (or other people significant to the child),

- existing foster carers, and

- new permanent carers who would initially be strangers to the child they are willing to care for.

Whatever the current status of the family, the great complexity of needs for any child who has been separated from his or her birth parents will have to be addressed. All families offering permanence therefore need to be sensitively and comprehensively assessed irrespective of whether they are existing carers or relatives or a "new" family. Appropriate versions of BAAF's Form PAR* are being developed which can be used for each of these since the assessment involved will in each case require a different perspective.

Relatives or other people significant to the child can offer the unique advantage to the child of maintaining them within their wider family network. This offers greater continuity of family heritage, history and relationships. However, the degree of

---

* The following BAAF forms can be used for assessments: Form PAR (Prospective Adopter's Report); Form C (Connected Persons) (for assessing friends and family); Form F Fostering (for assessing foster carers); Form ICA (for assessing intercountry adopters).

previous contact with the child can vary widely. Research (Sellick *et al*, 2004) has shown that such placements can be very successful. However, there may be particular issues around family dynamics, for example, in cases where relationships with birth parents have been poor or where the child has been sexually abused. The degree of preparation, training and support (including financial) which is available from the agency may play a significant part in both making and maintaining such placements.

Existing foster carers should go through a full reassessment and approval process which will give due weight to the child's permanence needs. Such carers may be seeking special guardianship, a residence order, a change to long-term fostering, or adoption. Within this assessment the developmental needs and age of the child, identity issues, cultural and ethnic needs, and the strength and quality of their existing attachments and community links will all play their part.

Guidance 3.25 specifies that: 'It should be made clear to foster carers, or those who apply to be approved for specific children, that their assessment will be in respect of their suitability as adopters generally and that, if they are approved, their suitability to adopt a specific child or children will be addressed separately as part of the matching process.'

New permanent carers will need assessments which identify clearly their understanding of the likely needs of children and their skills and experience which will enable them to meet these needs. The panel can give advice on the age, sex and the number and likely needs of children for whom the prospective adopter seems best suited.

It would be helpful for agency procedures and details of the assessment process in relation to the approval and use of any of these three groups to be added to the folder.

Timescales

Guidance 3.1 specifies that the following timescales should generally be complied with. However, it further states that:

Where the agency is unable to comply with a timescale or decides not to, it should record the reasons on the prospective adopter's case record. This might occur, for example, where

information needed by the agency is delayed, or where the prospective adopter and the agency agree that more time is needed to complete preparation or an assessment.

And it is required that:

- written information about the adoption process should be sent within **five working days** to the enquirers in response to their enquiry.

- the enquirers should be invited to an adoption information meeting or be offered an individual interview by the agency within **two months** of their enquiry.

- the adoption panel should receive all necessary information about the prospective adopter from the agency within **six weeks** of the completion of the report on the prospective adopter.

- the adoption panel's recommendation about the suitability of the prospective adopter to adopt a child should be made within **eight months** of the receipt of their formal application.

- The agency's decision on whether the prospective adopter should be approved as suitable to adopt should be taken within **seven working days** of receipt of the adoption panel's recommendation and final set of minutes (NMS 17.11).

- The prospective adopter should be informed orally of the agency's decision within **two working days** and written confirmation should be sent to them within **five working days** (Guidance 3.62).

Information required for a full report

The information required for a full report on a prospective adopter is detailed in the AAR Part 1 of Schedule 4 and in AAR 25. This includes the following.

Part 1 of Schedule 4

- Factual information such as date of birth, ethnicity, religion, etc. A photograph must be obtained.

- Whether he/she is domiciled or habitually resident in the British Islands. (These are England, Wales, Scotland, Channel Islands and the Isle of Man.) To be eligible to adopt in the UK at least one of a couple must be domiciled or both must have been habitually resident for not less than a year at the date of application for an adoption order.

- Personality and interests.

- Details of past relationships and current relationship with partner.

- A family tree.

- A chronology since birth.

- The applicant's observations on his/her experience of being parented.

- His/her parenting experience and an assessment of his/her parenting ability.

- A description of the wider family, their role and importance in relation to the applicant and to any future child.

- Information on the home, neighbourhood, friendships and social networks.

- Information on household members, including any children, whether living at home or not.

- Educational and employment history and current employment.

- Income and expenditure.

- Information on the applicant's capacity to meet a child's needs, share a child's history and understand and support a child with feelings of loss and trauma.

- The applicant's reasons for wanting to adopt, views and feelings about adoption, about parenting and his/her capacity to parent, views about a child's education, religious and cultural upbringing and about contact.

- The views of other members of the family, including extended family, about adoption.

AAR 25

- A summary by the agency's medical adviser on the health of applicants.

- Any relevant information from the area authority reference.

- Any observations in relation to the CRB checks and arising from preparation groups.

- The agency's assessment of the prospective adopter's suitability to adopt a child.

- Regulations specifically require that the agency must 'in determining the suitability of a couple to adopt a child, have proper regards to the need for stability and permanence in their relationship' (SAR 4(2)). This applies whether or not the couple are married.

- Towards the end of the process the agency is required to arrange a "second opinion" visit by a team manager or adoption worker who has not been involved with the assessment. Panel members should check whether this worker had any additional comments, if these are not detailed in the report.

- It will also be helpful if the report describes any adoption support and training needs which have already been identified for the family, with information on how it is planned to meet these.

- The report should describe any discussions which the prospective adopters and the agency workers have had about the range of children, in terms of age, numbers, likely needs and background for whom the prospective adopters would like to be considered. This should include the workers' analysis of their ability to meet the needs of children within this range and should include any difference of view about this between the prospective adopters and the workers.

- The prospective adopter must be shown this report and given ten days in which to comment. These comments should be available to the panel. A report using BAAF's Prospective Adopter's Report (Form PAR) or equivalent should cover all these issues.

In addition, the panel should receive:

- a written report on the referee interviews;

- the medical adviser will have the full medical reports but these will not be circulated to each panel member unless so advised by the medical adviser. The panel may, however, request further information which could include some or all of the detailed medical reports.

Checks and references required

See also information on references in Chapter 2.

- **Enhanced CRB checks** These should be renewed every two years (Guidance 3.74). There may also, exceptionally, be additional "soft information" from police checks. CRB checks are needed on any member of the household aged 18 or over. The Glossary to the Guidance states that "household" 'may include others who do not reside in the home but are considered by the agency to be members of the household as they often stay in or visit the home'.

Some specified offences automatically exclude applicants. These are mainly offences against children. Panels need to take into account any other offences which may have been committed and consider the implications of these for the adoption of children. Questions to explore include the nature of the offence, the age of the applicant at the time and how long ago this was, the applicant's honesty in disclosing the offence before the CRB check came in, his or her attitude to the offence now and whether he or she is still in touch with people who may still be offending. If an applicant has learnt and moved on, their past experience of offending may give them valuable empathy with a child whose birth parents have a history of offending. There is additional information in Chapter 2.

Applicants may have lived abroad for extended periods. Guidance 3.31 states that the agency 'must decide whether it should carry out any other checks or take up additional references. It should then decide whether it has sufficient information to justify proceeding with the prospective adopter's application.' Some agencies have found that contact with a local police authority in the country concerned has produced helpful information or confirmation that the applicant was not known. An employer's reference covering the period may also be helpful.

- **Any relevant information held by the local authority where the applicants live.** This should include information from children's services records, including child protection, and from education records (Guidance 1.48). It is for agencies to decide whether to get checks from any previous local authorities. Good practice would suggest that the previous ten years should be covered. It may also be helpful to do a check with a local authority where the applicant has jointly parented children with a previous partner.

- **Personal references.** There must be written reports on interviews with at least three personal referees, not more than one of whom may be a relative. It is helpful if, between them, referees have known each applicant for a considerable period of

time, as well as still being in close touch. For some applicants, it may be necessary to have information from more than the specified number of referees to achieve this. It can be helpful to have a reference from a relative in each partner's family, rather than from just one side of the family.

- **It can be helpful to have a reference from any adult children of either applicant.** It can also be helpful to have a reference from a former partner of either applicant, particularly if there has been joint parenting experience with the applicant. Agencies and panel members need to be clear what their policy is on this. Some ex-partners may be very bitter and angry still, and what they say must be considered in this context. It will be important to try to check any negative comments against the comments of adult children and/or personal referees. Where an applicant refuses to give the information which would allow the agency to contact an ex-partner, they should be asked to give reasons for this, e.g. that the ex-partner is violent and might pose a serious threat. As far as possible, these need to be checked against the comments of any adult children or referees. The agency and panel members will then need to make a judgement as to whether the lack of contact with an ex-partner is crucial to the consideration of the applicants or not.

The full prospective adopter's report

The assessing social worker will often share drafts of the report (PAR) with the applicants during the assessment so that they can check it for accuracy and can contribute to it. Once it is completed, AAR 25.8 requires that the prospective adopters are given a copy of the report, minus the references and medical report, and invited to make any comments within 10 days.

Panel members are then sent:

- the PAR;

- any comments made on it by the prospective adopters;

- written reports of the interviews with referees;

- the medical reports if advised by the medical adviser, but usually a summary by the medical adviser;

- any other relevant information.

Guidance 3.51 clarifies that additional "soft" information obtained from the police cannot be disclosed to the subject or to the panel but must be considered by the agency. If the panel requests additional information the agency should obtain it, so far as is reasonably practical and Guidance 3.52 makes clear that: 'Unless there is good reason to justify not doing so, additional information...should be shared with the prospective adopter'.

Legal advice

The panel is not required to obtain legal advice but may decide to do so. There could, for example, be issues around domicile and habitual residence or around checks on people who have lived abroad.

Conditional or "in principle" recommendations

Guidance makes clear that the decision-maker's decision must be based on a definite recommendation.

Panel members should ensure that all statutory checks and references are in place and up to date for prospective adopters and that there are no outstanding pieces of information needed. If there are, the panel will need to defer making a recommendation. The agency adviser to the panel is given responsibility (Guidance 1.40) in conjunction if necessary with the Chair, to "gatekeep" cases being presented to panel and to withdraw a case prior to panel if important information is missing.

Brief report

The agency does not need to complete a full report where it receives information that leads it to consider that the prospective adopter may not be suitable to adopt a child ((AAR 25(7) and SAR 5)).

This could be information from checks and references or from the health reports or it could be information gathered in the course of interviews by the assessing social worker. Guidance 3.54 specifies that the assessing social worker should seek advice from a manager and they should ensure that the prospective adopter is counselled about the issues of concern. Other professionals should be involved as appropriate 'for example, ensuring that health professionals counsel the applicant about information relating to their health'.

These discussions should clearly be as open and honest as possible. However, this may not always be possible. There may be concerning information about one applicant which their partner is unaware of. In this case, the agency may need to give the applicant the choice of telling their partner or of withdrawing, or, after discussion with the applicant concerned, the social worker may need to inform the couple that as a consequence of information obtained from the checks the joint application cannot proceed. Referees may have given concerning information in confidence. If this is the case, the agency should encourage the referee to agree that the concerns can be shared or, if this is not possible, should try and validate the information from other sources.

As a result of these discussions, applicants may decide to withdraw. However, if they do not, and if the agency decides that its concerns will not be alleviated by further work, it must prepare a brief report for panel. Applicants must be shown this report and given ten days to comment (AAR 25(8)). However, as is the case when a full report is prepared, Guidance 1.50 and 1.51 clarify that the health report, references and any additional information, e.g. "soft information" obtained from the police, are not shared.

The panel must consider the report and decide either to request the agency to prepare a full report or to recommend that the prospective adopter is not suitable to adopt a child (The Adoption and Children (Miscellaneous Amendments) Regulations 2005). Panel members will need to consider carefully the reasons, which should be detailed in the report, why the agency has taken the view that further work would not resolve the issues.

Given that the social worker and the applicants will not be in agreement on the best outcome, the panel may wish to consider a different process to that usually used. Some panels find it helpful to meet with the applicants first and then, separately, to meet with the social workers.

See later section in this chapter on the decision-making process.

Applicants attending the panel

The agency is required to invite prospective adopters to attend a meeting of the panel when their suitability as adopters is being considered (AAR

26(4)). Guidance 3.57 states that the purpose is 'to provide an opportunity for both the panel and the prospective adopter to discuss and clarify the prospective adopter's reasons for wishing to adopt, and any other matters that either party considers relevant to the application'. Applicants are not required to attend but it is to be hoped that they will be encouraged to do so. Many panels have virtually 100 per cent attendance by applicants, and both applicants and panel members have found the experience helpful. It is important that prospective adopters are well prepared and given information on who will be present and their roles and also on the panel process.

Applicants may wish to bring a supporter to panel with them. This can be helpful, particularly if the applicant is single. However, it should be made clear to everyone what the support person's role is and whether, for instance, they are permitted to speak. When applicants are in disagreement with the agency, as will be the case when a brief report is presented, it needs to be made clear that the support person, who could be a lawyer, is not there to speak for the applicants. There should be a clear and consistent policy, rather than this being decided on the day.

Many panels formulate their questions and then invite either the social worker in first and then the prospective adopters or both in together. Prospective adopters are usually asked to leave while panel members reach their recommendation. They may be told the recommendation immediately or, less frequently, their social worker may do this later.

It is important that panel members do not let a brief meeting with applicants take the place of a careful consideration of all the issues in the written reports. They need to consider how much weight to give to the attendance and performance of applicants at panel. Some may be much more used than others to talking in a large and fairly formal group. The weight of evidence as to whether people should be recommended for approval should be provided in the written reports. Nevertheless, if people appear very significantly different from the descriptions of them in the reports, this may require more investigation.

Feedback should be gathered from prospective adopters about their experience of attending panel

so that the panel can evaluate its performance and make any agreed changes.

BAAF publishes a useful pamphlet entitled *Prospective Adopters Attending Adoption Panel* (Lord, 2011).

Issues to consider

A family assessment should outline, on the basis of evidence, each family's particular strengths and limitations, the extent to which any concerns are acknowledged or shared by the family itself, and the family's potential for further development.

All family placements involve a careful balancing of the strengths and limitations which exist within each individual family. While the element of risk involved in making family placements for children can never be eliminated, it can be minimised by careful assessment, sound preparation and good support. It is also vital that the panel itself should encourage full acknowledgement, discussion and sharing of the risks involved for a placement, as well as acknowledging the potential demonstrated within each family. This should take place both at the time of considering approval and later, when matching with a child is being considered. All concerns, together with the reasons for these, should be openly voiced and shared. The need for any ongoing work with the family should be identified at the time of approval and the way in which the outcomes of this will be fed back to the panel.

Preparation, training and support

The prospective adopter's report presented to the panel should include details of the content of training already provided by the agency together with unmet training or developmental needs identified, and a clear timetable and plan for meeting these. What further information and support has been available to them pre-placement and what will be available post-placement? All families also need a commitment to continuing to learn about children's needs in the future as knowledge and practice develop. They need to be able to adapt to changes in the child's needs over time and as the child matures.

Strengths needed

The amount of time, energy and space available within each family's emotional and other commitments needs careful consideration. Both the support network and the family's ability to admit difficulties and to use professionals appropriately for support are important. Personal qualities necessary include being able to acknowledge needs from their own and the child's past, not to be rigid or judgemental, to be able to communicate well with children, and to be able to work with the unpredictable. Families should also be able to juggle many demands on their time, energy and resources, acknowledge and value diversity and difference, and be active in the promotion of continuity including a consideration of the child's heritage.

Issues relating to the family

Motivation

What is the applicant's motivation? For example, could it be to "rescue" a child or to meet high dependency needs? To overcome frustrations from their own past or to ensure another sibling in the family? Does the family "understand" its motivation to care for a child? What needs of their own are each of the family members trying to meet? Do they have realistic expectations of themselves? Can they acknowledge needs for support? Have they been encouraged to join any support groups such as Adoption UK (see Appendix 4) or a disability support group if relevant?

Relationship

How long have the couple been together? How stable and permanent does their relationship appear to be? Does either of them have a history of broken relationships? Have the couple weathered any stressful situations together? Regulations stipulate that the agency must consider carefully the 'stability and permanence in their relationship' (SAR 4(2)). Does it have the strength to withstand the demands of an adoption placement?

Unmarried couples can now, for the first time, apply jointly for an adoption order. "Couple" is defined in the Adoption and Children Act 2002 section 144(4) as 'a married couple', 'two people who are civil partners of each other' or 'two people (whether of different sexes or the same sex) living as partners in an enduring family relationship'. Section 144(5) of

the Adoption and Children Act 2002 spells out that this does not include two people one of whom is the other's parent, grandparent, sister, brother, aunt or uncle.

Infertility issues

Has a couple jointly worked through each partner's own pain and loss? What stage of the grieving process has each reached? Do the adults involved recognise that these feelings may be revived at times throughout their lives? Has each thought about their "fantasy child" and the possible impact of this on a child placed? How would each of them cope if a child were subsequently born to them? If there is no known reason for their infertility, are they prepared to use contraception in the early stages of a child's placement with them?

Health issues

The medical adviser will have a medical report, completed by the applicant's GP, and will have followed up any issues of concern with the GP and with any specialists involved. (The social worker preparing the assessment should liaise with the medical adviser about any health-related issues which come to light during the assessment. Particular care will be needed in handling what may be very sensitive and confidential information.)

The medical adviser should have an up-to-date, holistic and accurate report on the applicant's individual and family health history and current physical, emotional and mental health. This should include lifestyle factors which may have an impact on their ability to parent a vulnerable child. The medical adviser should assist the agency in assessing health and lifestyle risk factors which may affect the decision about the applicant's suitability to care for a child. It is very important that the medical adviser does not see the role as one of accepting or rejecting a particular applicant purely on health grounds. The medical adviser acts as an adviser to the panel, outlining the issues and risks and providing the available evidence base, so that the panel can discuss the case and make a recommendation.

It is important that agencies satisfy themselves that adopters have a reasonable expectation of retaining the health and vigour necessary to meet the physical and emotional needs of a growing child and to care for a child until he or she is grown up. Age is clearly relevant but more significant are specific medical conditions and health-related lifestyle factors such as smoking, alcohol consumption, diet and exercise, as well as looking at what positive factors prospective adopters have to offer a child.

The advice of the medical adviser on health issues will obviously be taken very seriously by other panel members, and eventually, by the agency decision-maker. However, it is important for panel members to be clear that they are jointly responsible for recommendations made to the agency. (See Chapter 2, *Agency policy and practice issues*, for more information on health-related lifestyle factors.) There is helpful additional information in BAAF's guide, *Doctors for Children in Public Care* (Mather and Batty, 2000).

Other children in the family

How well prepared are such children? Do the adults involved understand the considerable impact there will be on other children in the family? Can they give support to all the children in the family while dealing with conflicting needs or ambivalence from existing children? How well could they deal with difficulties for existing children such as jealousy or aggression towards them or involvement in sexualised behaviour? Research (Sellick *et al*, 2004) indicates that placing a child close in age to an existing birth child adds to the risk of placement breakdown. An age gap of at least two years is usually recommended.

Identity issues

What positive sense does the family have of the cultural, racial, religious and linguistic heritage and identity of its members? Where these are different, how does each member of the family acknowledge and understand and value the diversity represented? What is the social worker's assessment of these issues?

How open would this family be to a child's developing sexuality? In supporting a young person who may be lesbian or gay, what are the potential areas of difficulty the family envisages for itself?

The assessment process

Has the process adequately acknowledged and met the needs of all applicants, including those who are single people, those from black and minority ethnic groups, those with disabilities and those who are lesbian or gay? Has the preparation material been appropriate? Have any language or communication needs been suitably addressed? Have any physical requirements been adequately met? Is sufficient understanding and appreciation shown within the assessment of the family's culture, for example, for a deaf family? Has there been any involvement of workers who are appropriate to this family's needs within the assessment process?

Discrimination and racism

What understanding and experience do the applicants have of discrimination and racism? What strengths and coping skills do they have? What preparation and support will be available to them? Do they understand and adopt an anti-discriminatory approach to parenting and how is this demonstrated, including within their own family and social networks?

How well will this family be able to help a child placed with them? If they do not share the same ethnicity as the child, Guidance 4.7 states that 'The core issue is what qualities, experiences and attributes the prospective adopter can draw on and their level of understanding of the discrimination and racism the child may be confronted with when growing up'. Does a family which shares the child's ethnicity appreciate the additional tasks they may face, for example, as a result of earlier transracial or transreligious placements, including possible initial rejection by the child? Do single applicants, lesbian or gay applicants, or those with a disability appreciate that significant issues may arise for them because of the child's previous experiences of prejudice and discrimination?

Issues relating to meeting the child's needs

Unidentified needs at time of placement

Does the family realise that some issues may only be identified once the child is in a permanent placement? How will the family cope with areas of unexpected difficulty, for example, medical problems or undisclosed abuse? What support will there be for them?

The child's birth family

All prospective adopters will need to demonstrate understanding of the intense emotional needs of children who have, whatever their age, experienced separation from their birth parents and sometimes from their siblings as well.

Does the family understand and show compassion for the sorts of reasons why children cannot be cared for by their birth parents? Does the family demonstrate insecurity or feelings of ambivalence or rejection towards the varied backgrounds from which a child might come? What do family members feel about a child's family history of mental illness, criminal records, prostitution or alcoholism? Can they identify and value the positive without glossing over any difficulties?

Identifying and understanding the child's wishes and feelings

What importance does the family place on the child's wishes and feelings and how well are family members likely to be able to communicate with the child? Do they understand the pain and loss the child is likely to feel about separation from his or her birth family? Do they accept that, as a result, the child may feel confusion, ambivalence, anger or depression which may be reflected in his or her behaviour towards new carers? Will they be able to value and continue to help the child with life story work and "retell" the story appropriately as the child matures?

Attachment issues

Does the family acknowledge any limits that a child may show in his or her current ability to form meaningful and positive attachments? Do family members understand the reasons for this? Are their expectations of a child's ability to form new attachments to them realistic? Do they understand the importance of valuing and maintaining in some way links with people with whom the child has good attachments such as grandparents or previous foster carers? Do they understand the special importance of siblings for potential lifetime relationships?

Identity issues

Is there any work that needs to be done with the family before it can fully support and work with the child's sense of identity? Where a transracial

placement may be under consideration, how far can the family identify and meet the child's needs and how would they plan to actively fill in any "gaps" they may have in fully meeting the child's needs? What is the family's understanding of how their white identity will impact on their care of a black child? How will they help a black child deal with experiences of racism that they are ultimately unable to share?

Would a child feel comfortable in this family whatever his or her emerging sexuality may be?

Abuse and neglect issues

Does the family understand that they may only learn about some of the child's experiences and needs after placement? What help would family members anticipate giving the child themselves or seeking elsewhere? What future outcome do they expect for a child? Are there any issues in their own background which are relevant and how will they cope with the impact of these?

Behavioural issues

Does the family appreciate the wide range of difficult or disturbed behaviours it may have to cope with? How far do family members understand the impact that the child's previous life experiences will have on both the child and themselves? Is there any evidence of fixed ideas or rigidity around dealing with issues? How important is reward or punishment? How long can they cope when there is no evidence of progress?

Education issues

What is the family's understanding and expectation of children's educational development and the factors which impact on it? Do family members have unresolved issues from their own experiences such as academic expectations which are too high or too low or anxieties about special educational needs? How well could they support a child in difficulty and act as advocates with the school?

Health and disability issues

Disability needs to be considered in terms of the individual child's current development and developmental history, the family's own life experiences, the child's experience of discrimination, and the social context for the child. Can family members advocate for a child by seeking information and resources? Can they promote a child's welfare and independent abilities into adulthood? Can they deal with issues around identity and sexuality? Can they be satisfied with small achievements without underestimating the child's potential for larger ones?

Contact issues

Does the family understand the importance of both identifying and meeting the child's needs for contact, whether direct or indirect? What is their attitude towards contact generally, for example, where and when it should take place, and whether by agreement or court order? Are they open to reassessing and renegotiating a child's needs for contact over time? What support would they need and expect?

The needs of siblings

What understanding does the family show about the needs of siblings? Can family members consider and work with each child as an individual in his or her own right as well as a member of a sibling group? How well could they promote contact and attachment between siblings placed elsewhere, when appropriate? How would they deal with conflicting needs between siblings such as when some have parental contact and others not? Do they have skills, or a willingness to develop these, in working with siblings to promote positive and appropriate relationships with each other?

Range of approval

AAR 26 requires the panel only to make a recommendation about whether a prospective adopter is suitable to be an adoptive parent. However, many prospective adopters wish to be considered for a child or children within a particular age range and with specified needs and they will have been assessed and prepared with these in mind. Panels can give advice to the agency on a specific range of approval. Panel members should clarify whether there is any disagreement between the prospective adopters and the agency workers over the suggested approval range. Panel advice on the approval range 'will inform subsequent matching...although the agency is not restricted by such advice' (Guidance 3.60).

Agencies will need to decide how any changes to the approval range, which a panel has advised, will be made. This should be included in the agency's written procedures. It might be agreed that the decision-maker should have a role in this. It might also be agreed that any major change should be referred back to the panel for further advice.

Decision-making process

If, after the panel's recommendation, the decision-maker proposes not to approve the applicants (whether or not this accords with the panel's recommendation), he or she must notify the applicants in writing, giving reasons. This is called a "qualifying determination". If the panel's recommendation was different, i.e. a positive one, the applicants must be told this. The applicants then have 40 days in which to decide what to do. They can:

- **Accept the proposed decision.** A decision will be made at the end of 40 days or earlier if the applicants confirm in writing that they are withdrawing; OR

- **Make representations to the decision-maker.** He or she will probably receive written information and meet the applicants. He or she can decide whether or not to re-present the case to the panel. If it is, the panel must give the case fresh consideration and make a recommendation and the decision-maker must take this recommendation into account when making the decision, which is final; OR

- **Apply to the Independent Review Mechanism–Adoption and Fostering (IRM).** This has been operating since April 2004 in relation to adoption and was extended, from April 2009, to include fostering. It is operated by BAAF under contract to the DfE. It is an independent review process, conducted by a panel. Prospective or approved adopters and foster carers may apply to the IRM, following a 'qualifying determination' made on the basis of a full, or in the case of adopters only, a brief, report. They will be invited to attend an independent panel, set up in a similar way to an agency panel. The agency will send representatives to the panel too. The IRM panel will receive all the reports presented to the agency's panel and may request some additional information. It will not have a copy of the panel minutes. Its recommendation and minutes will go to the agency decision-maker, who will make the final decision. Fourteen adoption and 77 fostering applications were made to the IRM in the year April 2009 to March 2010. Nine of the adoption applications were from married couples and five from single women; 11 were working with local authorities and three with voluntary adoption agencies. None related to intercountry adoption. Of the 11 cases heard within the year, the IRM panels recommended approval in six cases. The agency decision-maker made a positive decision in four of these cases. The main reasons for recommending that applicants were not suitable to adopt were an inability to work with the agency and to understand the needs of looked after children, a lack of emotional resilience and a range of medical issues. The IRM noted a lack of evidence to support decisions in some cases and a need for robust risk assessments.

Review and termination of approval

Regulations require agencies to review the approval of prospective adopters until a child is placed. This must be done 'whenever the adoption agency considers it necessary' but otherwise at least annually (AAR 29(2)). The case only needs to be referred to the panel if the agency proposes to terminate approval. If this is the case, it must prepare a report giving its reasons. The prospective adopter must be given 10 days to comment on this before it goes to panel. Good practice would suggest that the prospective adopter is invited to attend panel and arguably this is required by AAR 26(4). The panel makes a recommendation, having requested further information if required. The decision-making process is then as already described, with the prospective adopter having the right to apply to the IRM.

A review should be held if the agency has serious concerns about prospective adopters and also after any significant event such as a couple separating, a new health issue, a pregnancy or a disrupted placement.

What next?

A panel recommends that applicants are suitable to be adoptive parents and the agency makes a decision about this. The panel may then not hear about the prospective adopters again until a matching with a child is presented. These matches are usually presented to the panel of the child's agency and so a voluntary adoption agency panel may have no further involvement after its initial recommendation.

It is important that agency staff have regular contact with approved adopters who are waiting to be matched with a child. Panels should receive regular brief updating reports, perhaps every three or six months, which would give the conclusion of reviews and detail any changes made to advised approval ranges. They should check on whether families have been referred to the Adoption Register and be put in touch with Adoption UK, the self-help group for adoptive and prospective adoptive parents (see Appendix 4).

References

Lord J (2011) *Prospective Adopters Attending Adoption Panel*, London: BAAF

Mather M and Batty D (2000) *Doctors for Children in Public Care: A resource guide advocating, protecting and promoting health*, London: BAAF

Sellick C, Thoburn J and Philpot T (2004) *What Works in Adoption and Foster Care?*, London: Barnardo's/BAAF

Families offering placements – from first enquiry to approval

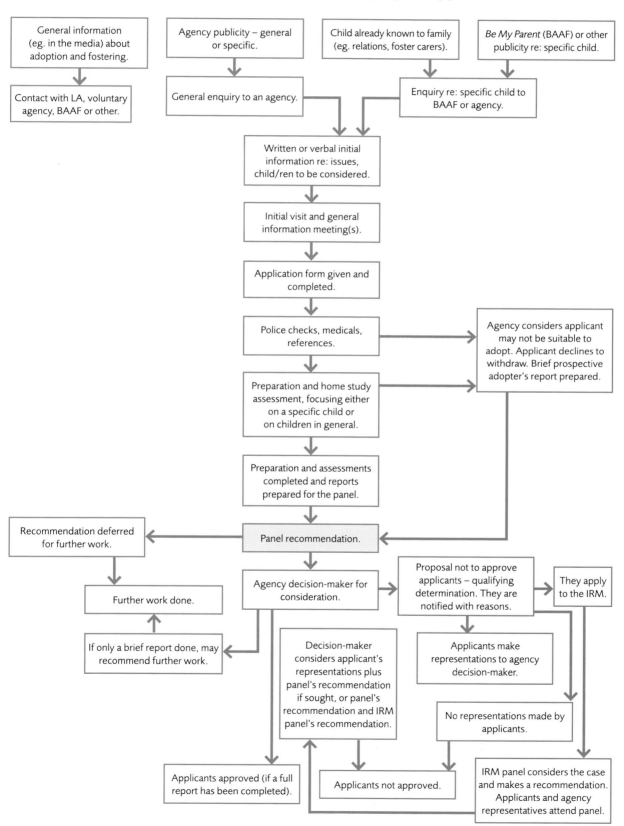

5 Matching children with families

Panel functions

Regulation 32 of the Adoption Agencies Regulations 2005 requires the panel to consider and to recommend 'whether the child should be placed for adoption with that particular prospective adopter'.

It must also consider and may give advice to the agency about:

(a) *the authority's proposals for the provision of adoption support services for the adoptive family;*

(b) *the arrangements the adoption agency proposes to make for allowing any person contact with the child; and*

(c) *whether the parental responsibility of any parent or guardian or the prospective adopter should be restricted and, if so, the extent of any such restriction.*

The panel must have regard to the duties imposed by section 1 of the Adoption and Children Act 2005 ("the welfare checklist") when considering its recommendation. See Chapter 2 for information on this.

The decisions about the adoption plan for the child and about the suitability of the prospective adopters will probably already have been made. However, one or both of those recommendations can be made at the same time as the matching recommendation.

Matching considerations draw very heavily on the work that will have been done already in identifying a child's needs and deciding on a plan and in assessing and preparing a family and identifying their strengths and limitations. It will probably be helpful, therefore, to refer back to Chapters 3 and 4, *Considering adoption for a child* and *Families offering placements.*

The flow chart at the end of this chapter, *Process for identifying a family and making a match after a decision that a child should be placed for adoption,* might also be helpful.

Process by which the proposed match has reached the panel

Proposed matches are made in a variety of ways:

- The family may have been identified from the agency's own waiting list of approved families.

- If none of the agency's own approved families seemed suitable, a link may have been made with a family already approved by another agency. This could have been done by referral to the local consortium to which the agency belongs, by referral to the Adoption Register for England & Wales or by referral to a family finding service such as BAAF's *Be My Parent* newspaper or Be My Parent online or *Children who wait.* There may have been direct contact with other agencies or the child's need for a family may have been publicised in the press.

- The family may have been recruited and assessed with this specific child in mind, probably by responding to publicity for the child before they had started the assessment process.

- The family may be the child's current foster carers.

- The family may know the child in some other way, for example, as a family member or as a friend or a teacher. They will have been assessed and approved with this particular child in mind.

The child's social worker may have had more than one family to consider. He or she will have read their reports and met the families and their workers often with the adoption worker who is family finding for the child. The child's foster carer or residential social worker may well have met the families too. Those involved will have considered what each family has to offer to this particular child and their potential to provide a stable and permanent family for him or her. Guidance 4.22 makes it clear that: 'The agency is responsible for considering and comparing alternative prospective adopters for a particular child. In its report to the panel on the proposed placement, the agency should only propose one adoptive family (that is, one couple or a single person) as the prospective adopter(s).'

AAR 31 requires that, when the agency has decided which family to proceed with, they must give them a copy of the child's permanence report and any other relevant information. This could include photos and a video of the child. They must then meet with the prospective adopters and ascertain their views on the placement and on the proposed arrangements for ongoing contact with members of the birth family or others.

If the agency and the adopters are then keen to proceed with a match, the agency must carry out an assessment of the needs of the child, the prospective adopters and any other children whom they may have, for adoption support services.

Timescales

Guidance 4.1 specifies that:

> The following timescales apply where the agency proposes to place a child with the prospective adopter, whether the prospective adopter is resident in the UK or abroad:
>
> - a proposed placement with a suitable prospective adopter should be identified and approved by the panel within **six months** of the agency deciding that the child should be placed for adoption;
>
> - where a parent has requested that a child aged under six months be placed for adoption, a proposed placement with a suitable prospective adopter should be identified and approved by the panel within **three months** of the agency deciding that the child should be placed for adoption;
>
> - the agency's decision on whether to approve a proposed placement with a suitable prospective adopter should be taken within **seven working days** of the receipt of the adoption panel's recommendation and final set of panel minutes. (NMS 17.11)

Guidance is clear that, although these timescales should generally be adhered to, the paramount consideration must always be the welfare of the child. Where the agency is unable to comply with a timescale or decides not to, the reasons for this should be recorded on the child's case record.

AAR 32(5) allows a panel to make a matching recommendation at the same panel meeting as recommends the plan for the child and the approval of the adopter. However, usually this will already have been done.

Authorisation to place for adoption

Before a child can be placed for adoption the agency must have one of the following:

- a placement order made by a court;

- formal consent from the birth parent(s) witnessed by a CAFCASS officer;

- agreement by the birth parent(s) to place an infant under the age of six weeks. There is a prescribed form for this written agreement at the end of Chapter 2 of the Guidance.

Panel members should ensure that at least one of these is in place or is planned. A placement order can be made if the grounds for making a care order are met or if the child has no parent or guardian. The court can simply make a placement order. However, in most cases it will be better if it first makes a care order. This will be suspended while the placement order is in force, but will be reinstated should the placement order be revoked before the child is adopted.

Formal consent to placement for adoption can only be given once a child is at least six weeks old. This can be consent to placement with identified adopters, consent to placement with any adopters chosen by the agency or consent to the latter should the child be removed from or returned by the identified adopters.

Information required

Panel members should expect to have up-to-date and fully completed copies of the following reports.

On the child

- A copy of the child's permanence report. This should include updated information as necessary to ensure that it gives an accurate account of the current situation.

- The permanence report will include a health summary by the medical adviser and he or she will also have the full health reports available on the child and birth family members. Other panel members are entitled to see these if they wish.

- Possibly other relevant specialist reports to ensure a comprehensive picture of the child's needs.

- Minutes of the panel meeting which recommended that the child should be placed for adoption, including any advice on contact arrangements.

On the family

- The prospective adopter's report (BAAF's Form PAR can be used).

- The adopter's report will include a summary of their health by the medical adviser. He or she will also have full medical reports available. In most cases, Form AH should remain valid for two years. However, BAAF recommends that medical advisers telephone the GP for an informal update if a child is to be placed more than six months after the prospective adopters' medical examination.

- Minutes of the panel meeting which recommended approval and the panel's advice on approval range. It should be noted that Guidance 3.60 comments that research indicates that "stretching" of adopter's preferences puts placements at higher risk of difficulties.

The adoption placement report

AAR 31 requires that an adoption placement report is written, to include the following:

- The agency's reasons for proposing the placement.

- The views of the prospective adopter about the proposed placement and the proposed arrangements for contact with birth relatives or others.

- The agency's proposals for the provision of adoption support services to the adoptive family. (Where the agency is a voluntary adoption agency, it is recommended that it seeks, and includes in the report, any proposals the relevant local authority may have.)

- The arrangements the agency proposes to make for allowing any person contact with the child.

The prospective adopter must have been given a copy of the child's permanence report to read, plus any other information which the agency considers

relevant. Proposed contact arrangements must have been discussed with them, and there must also have been an assessment of the adoption support needs of the family. Guidance 4.24 makes clear that: 'It is unacceptable for agencies to withhold information about a child and provide a picture that bears little relation to the reality'.

The prospective adopter must also have been given a copy of the placement report and ten days in which to comment, before the reports go to panel. Any comments made, if not incorporated into the report, should be given to panel.

It can also be helpful to have a brief summary of how family finding was done, how this particular family was found, and whether any other families were considered.

Guidance 4.25 states that: 'It is good practice for the medical adviser to meet with the prospective adopter to share all appropriate health information, to discuss the needs of the children...and to provide a written report of this meeting'.

Legal advice

The panel is not required to obtain legal advice for a matching but may do so. Legal factors may have changed since the plan for the child was considered. For example, birth parents might now have a different attitude to the adoption plan or different wishes about contact.

Attendance at the panel

The child's worker, and if possible his or her manager, and the family's worker should be present. It may also be helpful if the child's carer can attend for part of the discussion. Many panels invite prospective adopters to attend panel at this stage. It may be particularly helpful to discuss with them their views on proposed adoption support arrangements, on contact and on the exercise of their parental responsibility for the child after placement.

It is not usual for either the child or his or her birth parents to attend. However, it is important that panel members are fully informed about their views and wishes in relation to adoptive families in general and to this particular family if they have information about them. They could be invited to write or send an audiotape to panel members or to the Chair, if they wish.

Welfare of children

The panel, like the agency, is bound by the duties set out in section 1 of the Adoption and Children Act 2002. This is given in full in Chapter 2, and should be the overarching context in which the match for a child is considered.

Issues to consider

The art of making permanent placements appears to be in learning what the new parents have to give and what they will expect in return, and matching these with what the child needs and is willing to take from the new parents, and also what the child can give back to them. (Sellick and Thoburn, 1996)

No match will be "perfect" and panel members need to clarify and weigh up the risks and limitations as well as the strengths of the proposed match and to consider the adoption support services being proposed post-placement to try and minimise the risks.

The following list indicates some of the issues that panel members will need to consider. It is not intended to be exhaustive and other issues will need to be addressed in individual cases. Panel members should remember that they are not re-considering the approval of the family; they are considering whether the family can meet the needs of this particular child or sibling group.

The child's birth family

Panel members will need to check whether there have been any significant changes in the views or circumstances of birth family members since the plan for the child was recommended. Are there any particular factors, for example, the mental illness of a parent, which the prospective adopters may find difficult to accept? Is the family able to understand and accept the child's history?

In appropriate circumstances the proposed placement will...have been discussed with the child's birth family and their views should be included in the [placement] report. (Guidance 4.29)

The child's current understanding of and feelings about the past and about what is planned

Panel members will need to ask about the progress of the direct work that is being done with the child and about how ready the child is to move to a new family. How long has the child been waiting and how has he or she coped with this? Do the prospective adopters understand that the child will probably continue to need help for a long time to make sense of what has happened and to sort out his or her feelings toward their birth family? How able will the family be to help the child with this and what outside support will be available? What sort of family is the child envisaging? If this family is different, for example, a single parent when the child has assumed that he or she will have two parents, what work is being done to prepare the child?

The views of the child about the proposed placement are not required to be included in the placement report but 'where this has been discussed with the child, and particularly where the child already knows the prospective adopter (perhaps as their current foster carer), this will be relevant information to be included in the report' (Guidance 4.29).

Identity issues

Section 1 of the Adoption and Children Act 2002 requires that 'in placing the child for adoption the adoption agency must give due consideration to the child's religious persuasion, racial origin and cultural and linguistic background'.

Guidance 4.4 makes clear that active family finding should take place, seeking families in-house, from other adoption agencies, both local authorities and voluntary adoption agencies, and through the Adoption Register. This should put the child in an excellent position of being placed quickly with a new, safe and loving family. **If the prospective adopter can meet most of the child's needs, the social worker must not delay placing a child with the prospective adopter because they are single, older than other adopters or do not share the child's racial or cultural background** (emphasis in the original).'

Guidance 4.7 continues:

A prospective adopter can be matched with

a child with whom they do not share the same ethnicity, provided they can meet the child's other identified needs. The core issue is what qualities, experiences and attributes the prospective adopter can draw on and their level of understanding of the discrimination and racism the child may be confronted with when growing up.

Where the proposed new parents are not of the same cultural, ethnic, religious and linguistic background as the child, panel members will need to ask what efforts have been made to find such a family, and whether, with appropriate support, the family can nevertheless meet the child's needs. Does the family live in an ethnically diverse area? Do they have family members or friends of the same ethnicity as the child? If the proposed placement is to be recommended, what efforts are to be made by the family and the agency to actively meet the child's needs?

Guidance 4.8 says:

All families should help children placed with them to understand and appreciate their background and culture. Where the child and prospective adopter do not share the same background, the prospective adopter will need flexible and creative support to be given by their agency. This should be in the form of education and training, not just simplistic advice, provided in a vacuum, on learning their children's cultural traditions or about the food/cooking from their birth heritage. The support plan should consider how the child's understanding of their background and origin might be enhanced. This can include providing opportunities for children to meet others from similar backgrounds, and to practise their religion – both in a formal place of worship and in the home. Maintaining continuity of the heritage of their birth family is important to most children; it is a means of retaining knowledge of their identity and feeling that although they have left their birth family they have not abandoned important cultural, religious or linguistic values of their community.

Attachment issues

It will be very important for panel members to try and assess whether the proposed family has understood the long-term implications for the child and for his or her relationship with them of the child's early attachment experience. Does the family have realistic expectations of the child's ability to make an attachment to them?

Abuse and neglect issues

Does the family understand that the child may well have experienced more abuse than is currently known about? Are family members prepared, for instance, for the child to disclose previous sexual abuse once they are settled in their new family? Are there any issues in the family members' own backgrounds which are relevant here and how will they cope with the impact of these?

Behavioural issues

It will be helpful for panel members to check whether the proposed family has met the child's current carers to hear first hand about what the child is like to live with. (This would not involve the child in any way.) Is there any aspect of the child's behaviour that is likely to be particularly difficult for the new family? Is their approach to parenting and to discipline very different from that which the child is used to? How will they deal with the child's possible confusion about this?

Health and disability issues

The medical adviser will be able to discuss with other panel members issues relating to the health of the child and of their birth parents, and the implications of these for the proposed placement. The medical adviser may have already discussed these issues with the proposed adopters. Panel members will need to be sure that the prospective adopters understand the implications of uncertainties or gaps in the health information as well as of known factors. The medical adviser will be able to discuss with other panel members any health or disability issues in the prospective adoptive family and the implications of these for the particular child being matched. The medical adviser will also be able to outline the services which are likely to be needed to meet the child's health and disability needs in the future.

Education issues

Panel members will need to be clear that the prospective adopters have been given information about and understand the educational needs of the child. It will be helpful for the adopters to meet with the child's teachers and panel members should check whether this has already happened or is planned after the formal matching. Are there any particular factors in this child's educational needs which may be difficult for this family to meet? What are the facilities in their area and are any necessary specialist resources available?

The needs of siblings

It will be important to consider whether the proposed placement seems likely to meet the particular needs of each sibling in the group. Guidance 4.12 states that: 'Siblings should be adopted by the same prospective adopter unless there is good reason why they should not be. Where an agency is making a placement decision on two or more children from the same family it should be based on a comprehensive assessment of the quality of the children's relationship, their individual needs and the likely capacity of the prospective adopter to meet the needs of the siblings being placed together.'

Other children in the new family

Research (Sellick and Thoburn, 1996) clearly indicates that it is risky to place children too close in age to existing children in a family. An age gap of at least two years is suggested. Proposed matches with smaller age gaps will need to be carefully considered. Are there particular factors about the needs of the existing children and the needs of the child to be placed which are likely to be incompatible?

The family's feelings and expectations

It may be helpful if panel members ask why the family feels that they would be right for this particular child and that this particular child would be right for them. What are each family member's expectations of how the child will fit into their family and relate to them? Does this match with what is known about the child's needs and wishes and capacity to form relationships?

Adoption support services

The adoption placement report must include the local authority's proposals for providing adoption support services to the adoptive family and the adoption panel is required to consider these. (If the family has been approved by a voluntary adoption agency, the adoption support that this agency will offer should also be described.) The panel should also have any comments that the prospective adopters have made on the proposals. The placing local authority is responsible for assessing for and arranging the provision of adoption support services for three years after the adoption order. Any regular financial support agreed before the adoption order is made remains their responsibility long term.

Adoption support services are likely to be crucial to the success of the placement. There will almost certainly be some limitations and risks in any match as well as strengths, and panel members will need to check on the particular help that is planned to compensate in these areas. What help and support are proposed, and from whom, both after placement and after adoption? It is particularly important to check on this in interagency placements and in cases when the family may live outside the child's home area. What is the family's attitude to seeking help and to working with others, for instance, specialist therapists, whose help the child may need? Are the agency and family aware that support and help may be needed in the future even though this is not apparent at the time of placement? How will a need for help in the future be met? Panel members should check on the availability of specialist educational and medical facilities which may be necessary. The medical adviser will have a continuing role until the child is adopted and this can be helpful. Is a prospective adopter planning to give up work or take extended leave? What is the likely impact on the family of this?

Financial issues

These must be considered as part of adoption support services.

ASR 8 sets out the circumstances in which financial support may be paid to an adoptive parent. These include:

(a) *where it is necessary to ensure that the adoptive parent can look after the child;*

(b) *where the child needs special care which requires greater expenditure of resources by reason of illness, disability, emotional or behavioural difficulties or the continuing consequences of past abuse or neglect;*

(c) *where it is necessary for the local authority to make any special arrangements to facilitate the placement or the adoption by reason of*
- *the age or ethnic origin of the child*
- *the desirability of the child being placed with the same adoptive parents as his brother or sister (whether of full or half-blood) or with a child with whom he previously shared a home;*

d) *where such support is to meet the recurring costs in respect of travel for the purpose of visits between the child and a related person.*

The support given cannot normally include remuneration. However, **foster carers who apply to adopt a child in their care** can continue to be paid the same amount as they received as foster carers, including any remuneration they received. This remuneration element will usually cease to be paid from two years after the adoption order 'unless the local authority considers its continuation to be necessary having regard to the exceptional needs of the child or any other exceptional circumstances' (ASR 9).

There must usually be an assessment of the prospective adopter's means before financial support is agreed. However, the local authority *may* disregard means in the situations outlined in b), c) and d) above, when considering the payment of remuneration to a former foster carer, as described above, and when considering the initial costs of accommodating an agency adoptive child – a "settling-in grant".

Contact arrangements

The adoption placement report must include the agency's proposals for allowing any person contact with the child and the panel is required to consider these. The panel should also have any comments made by the prospective adopter.

Panel members should note that AAR 45(2) removes the general duty in the 1989 Children Act to promote contact. When an agency is authorised to place a child for adoption,

> *... there should be no general presumption for or against contact. This is why Regulation 45.2 of the Adoption Agencies Regulations 2005 (AAR) removes the general duty in the 1989 Act to promote contact. Contact between adopted children and their birth families can be beneficial, but research has also highlighted that any form of contact needs careful planning and support, and that children's views and their needs for contact may change over time so any contact plans must be kept under review.* (Guidance 7.1 and 7.2)

Contact with birth family members and other people significant to the child after placement can be contentious and panel members should clarify the child's needs for ongoing contact and the proposed family's willingness and ability to meet these needs. What actual contact is planned and with whom? A child's need for contact will probably change over time, and the family's flexibility on this should be clarified. What help and support will the agency give over managing contact? Will agency workers be available to help renegotiate contact in the future if this becomes necessary?

Contact after placement may be through letters and cards exchanged via the adoption agency by the adoptive family and birth family members or there may be face-to-face contact. Contact arrangements need to be considered not only for birth parents but for grandparents and other relatives and for siblings placed elsewhere (AAR 46 and 47 and Guidance 7.18–29, both deal with contact).

Parental responsibility

The panel must consider and may give advice to the agency about whether the parental responsibility of any parent or guardian or the prospective adopter should be restricted and if so the extent of any such restriction.

For the first time, under the Adoption and Children Act 2002, adoptive parents are given parental responsibility for the child on placement, rather than on the making of the adoption order, as before. They share this with the local authority and with any birth parent or guardian who has parental responsibility. The local authority has the power to restrict the parental responsibility of any parent, guardian or prospective adopter.

It will be helpful if the agency includes in the adoption placement report its proposals, if any, for any restrictions. It is likely that the exercise of parental responsibility by any parent or guardian has already been considerably restricted and will probably be even more so once the child is placed for adoption, although they will not lose it until the child is adopted. In coming to a view on any restriction on the prospective adopter's exercise of their parental responsibility, the agency and the panel should take account of the views of the prospective adopter, of the child, if he or she is of sufficient age and understanding and of anybody else which could include the birth parents or other relatives. Guidance 5.20 suggests that: 'It may well be appropriate for there to be a gradual "shift of power" so that the prospective adopter comes to have a greater degree of autonomy as the placement progresses and their confidence and parenting skills develop, bearing in mind that once the adoption order is made they alone will have parental responsibility'.

Baby placements where the child is relinquished for adoption

Birth parents are not able to consent formally to adoption until the infant is at least six weeks old. However, a baby younger than this can be placed for adoption provided the parent(s) have given their agreement to this in writing (AAR 35 (3), (4)). There is a prescribed form for this agreement at the end of Guidance Chapter 2. Once the baby is six weeks old, the agency must arrange for the parent(s)' formal consent to adoption, under section 19 of the Adoption and Children Act 2002. The consent, on a prescribed form, must be witnessed by a CAFCASS officer.

Guidance 2.47 suggests that, when parents have been counselled and adoption is considered the preferred adoption, the agency should start work on the permanence report. It should:

> ... arrange for the agency medical adviser and adoption panel to be ready to consider the case as soon as possible after the child is born. In some cases it may be feasible with enough preparation for the adoption panel to be ready to consider the case within a day or so of the birth and the agency decision-maker to make the decision the same day.

A placement before the child is six weeks old should only be made following further counselling of the parent(s) after the birth. Adoptive parents will need to be well prepared for the risk of the parent(s) changing their minds before the child

is six weeks old, in which case the baby would return to them (unless there were grounds for care proceedings.) They will also need to be prepared for health issues to emerge as the infant develops. However, if prospective adopters are prepared to take these risks, the benefit to the infant of a very early placement could be considerable. There is useful discussion of issues in BAAF's Good Practice Guide *Right from the Start: Best practice in adoption planning for babies* (Cousins, 2003).

Reaching a recommendation on a proposed match

As described earlier, prospective adopters will have been given quite a lot of information about the child. They may have met the foster carers, their adoption support needs will have been assessed, and they may, for example, have visited possible schools. The match can feel like a fait accompli. However, panel members have a responsibility to make a recommendation with, as always, the child's welfare throughout his or her life as their paramount consideration. Declining to recommend a match must remain a possible option.

What next?

A panel recommends whether a child should be placed for adoption with that particular prospective adopter and the agency then makes a decision about this. There is no provision for prospective adopters to make representations or to apply to the IRM if the match is not agreed.

Panel members should receive regular, perhaps three-monthly, reports on children placed but not yet adopted. Unfortunately, not all placements will work out successfully. Statistics from the research described in *Permanent family placement: A decade of experience* (Fratter *et al*, 1991) showed that an average of 21 per cent of the permanent placements in their sample disrupted. However, the child's age at placement was a very significant factor with, for instance, only six per cent of placements of children aged 3–4 disrupting; 17 per cent of those placed aged 5–8; 34 per cent of those placed aged 9–11; and 41 per cent of those placed aged 12–14. Panel members should have the opportunity to consider and learn from placements which disrupt (see Chapter 2, *Agency policy and practice issues*).

Process for identifying a family after a decision that a child should be placed for adoption

In the event of a placement disrupting, good practice suggests that the family's approval should be suspended. If the family wishes to be considered for a further placement, the agency should arrange a review to consider this. There is no requirement to refer the case to panel unless the agency is considering a termination of approval. In this case, the agency should follow the procedures set out in regulations for considering new applicants, i.e. the family should see the new report before it is presented to panel and should have 10 days in which to comment. They will also have an opportunity, following the panel's recommendation, should the decision-maker be minded to terminate their approval, to make representations either to him or her or to the IRM. Panel members should also consider whether any further work is needed with the child to enable him or her to benefit from a further placement for adoption. Exceptionally, panel members may be asked to consider a change of plan for the child.

References

Cousins J (2003), *Right from the Start: Best practice in adoption planning for babies*, London: BAAF

Fratter J, Rowe J, Sapsford D and Thoburn J (1991) *Permanent Family Placement: A decade of experience*, London: BAAF

Sellick C and Thoburn J (1996) *What Works in Family Placement?*, London: Barnardo's

6 Intercountry adoption

Introduction

Adoption in the UK is principally a service for children in the UK who need to be adopted and for those families coming forward to offer them a home. There are still many children being looked after by local authorities who are waiting for adoptive families and the focus of adoption work is still to work with these children and to recruit, prepare and support new families for them. For many years a very small number of looked after children have been placed for adoption with relatives living overseas. Now, for the first time, legislation enables local authorities to identify some children whose needs may be met by adoption overseas even though no family is yet identified. The panel has a role in this and the process is described later in this chapter.

However, the majority of intercountry adoption cases being considered by panel are likely to be of prospective adopters in the UK wanting to adopt a child from overseas. All local authorities have a duty to ensure that a service is offered to these prospective adopters. However, some have arrangements with a local voluntary adoption agency which is registered to do this work, to do so on their behalf. There is usually a charge to the applicants for the work involved in the completion of a prospective adopter's report. This varies but many agencies charge around £6,000. Many families want or only feel able to parent a young child without special needs and it is these families, among others, who often decide to try and adopt from overseas. The number of adoptions from overseas has remained fairly stable over the last few years at around 300 each year.

BAAF's position on intercountry adoption is that:

In believing that all children should, wherever possible, be brought up within their family of origin or within a family of the same "race", culture and nationality, BAAF supports international efforts to improve the lot of children and families in developing countries. However, we recognise that this can often be accomplished only in the long term, and that in the short term intercountry adoption will meet the needs of some children. We wish to ensure that adoptions are arranged according to the highest possible professional standards, with everything possible done to protect the interests of the children involved.

Intercountry adoption can arouse strong feelings and does raise genuine moral and ethical dilemmas. There is a need for panel members to have time to discuss and address these. However, this is best achieved in a separate session, away from consideration of individual cases.

Agency policies and procedures

The agency will need to decide the following issues:

- whether to undertake intercountry adoption home studies itself or to arrange for a voluntary agency to do them for people in its area;

- whether to make a charge and, if so, how much and whether to have any exemptions to charging, e.g. for relatives;

- how existing agency policies that address the importance of assessing adoptive parents whose culture, "race", religion and language match the child's as closely as possible will be taken into account;

- how policies on the importance for children of knowledge of their background and of some form of continuity with their past will be taken into account.

Considering and deciding whether a child should be placed for adoption outside the British Islands

(The British Islands are England, Wales, Scotland, Northern Ireland, the Channel Islands and the Isle of Man.)

For many years, arrangements have been made for some looked after children to be placed for adoption with families living overseas who are relatives of the child or known to them in some other way. This will still be possible, but under current legislation it is also possible, for the first time, for an agency, after a recommendation from the panel, to decide that a looked after child should be placed with a family living overseas even though no family has yet been identified. These latter placements must be made under the Hague Convention.

The "Hague Convention"

This is the shorthand description of the Convention on Protection of Children and Co-operation in respect of Intercountry Adoption. It was concluded in The Hague (Netherlands) in May 1993 and was finally ratified by the UK on 1 June 2003. Many other countries have ratified and implemented the Convention and new ones are doing so regularly. There are notable exceptions though, including the USA. It is possible to check on whether the Convention is in force in a particular country on www.hcch.net.

Considering whether a child should be placed for adoption in a Hague Convention country

Panel involvement in considering the plan

The panel is required to consider the adoption plan for the child under AAR 18 and The Adoptions with a Foreign Element Regulations (FER) 39 as it would for a child to be adopted in the UK. (See Chapter 3 for all the information required and the issues to be considered.) However, *in addition*, the panel must ensure that:

- 'The child has been counselled about the adoption plan and that it has been explained to the child in an appropriate manner the procedures in relation to, and the implications of, an adoption in an overseas country' (FER 36 and AAR 13). The child must have had this information confirmed in writing.

- The child's birth parents must also have been counselled and must have had the implications of, and the procedures for, an intercountry adoption explained to them. This must have been confirmed in writing (FER 37 and AAR 14).

- The child's permanence report must include

    - *a summary of the possibilities for placement within the UK* (FER 38(a))
    - *an assessment of whether an adoption by a person in a particular receiving state is in the child's best interests* (FER 38(b) and AAR 17).

If no particular family has been identified at this stage, the panel will need to enquire very closely into what family-finding efforts have been made to explore the possibilities for placement within the UK. It is probable that positive recommendations are likely to be considered in cases where this will enable a child to be placed with adopters overseas who match the child's ethnicity and heritage. For instance, for a child born to people visiting the UK or living in the UK but retaining strong links to their country of origin, it might well be appropriate to consider adoption for the child with adopters in that country.

Possibly most of the positive recommendations made, however, will be in relation to children for whom a family in a Convention country has already been identified, i.e. relatives or someone known to the child.

Panel members should ensure that they check on how any contact arrangements will be organised. These may, of course, be facilitated by a placement in the country where most of the child's birth relatives live.

Issues of adoption support should also be considered. The Adoption Support Services Regulations 2005 will not apply overseas although financial support agreed could still be given by the child's agency.

When the panel is considering an intercountry adoption under the Convention it must consider and take into account:

- the Article 15 report (on the prospective adopters) if available, and the agency's observations on this (FER 39); and

- the assessment in the child's permanence report on whether an adoption by a person in a particular country is in the child's best interests.

What happens next?

When the panel has made a recommendation about whether or not a child should be placed for adoption in accordance with the Convention, a decision is made by the agency in the usual way. Notification is sent to the Department for Education (DfE) which is the Central Authority for England. The DfE will then arrange for brief anonymised details of the child to be placed on its Convention list of children in England available for intercountry adoption.

If the child's adoption agency subsequently decides that adoption overseas is no longer appropriate, it must notify the DfE, which will withdraw the child's name from the Convention list. Although there is no requirement for the panel to be involved in rescinding the plan, it would be good practice for the panel to be notified and agencies might choose to seek the panel's advice on changing the plan.

When an approved prospective adopter living in a Convention country outside the British Islands wishes to adopt a child from England, their country's Central Authority will forward their papers to the DfE. The DfE will check their details and will then consult the list of waiting children. It will look at the age and gender of the child and whether the child is part of a sibling group. The DfE will not be able to consider any additional details.

If there are any children available for adoption who appear, at face value, to link with the characteristics of the child the prospective adopters are approved to adopt, the DfE will send their papers to the child's agency.

The child's agency must consider the papers in the same way as any other match. If they need additional information, they must request this via the DfE. If they decide to pursue the match, it must be presented to panel, as described in the next section.

If the child's local authority decides not to pursue the match, it must return the papers to the DfE. The DfE will hold papers on families for six months before returning them to their agency overseas. They can be resubmitted at the request of the adopters.

The panel's involvement in considering a match with approved adopters from a Hague Convention country

The agency will have received a full report on the prospective adopters, prepared in their country. This is referred to as an *Article 15* report as it is prepared under Article 15 of the Hague Convention.

The adoption panel is required by FER 44 to consider the match under AAR 32 as it would for a domestic match. (See Chapter 5 for all the information required and the issues to be considered. The Article 15 report will take the place of the prospective adopter's report.) The agency

must include their observations on the Article 15 report.

Panel members will need to give particular consideration to any arrangements for adoption support. The Adoption Support Services Regulations 2005 will not apply in the overseas country. However, any financial support agreed can continue to be paid by the child's agency.

Panel members will also need to be clear how any arrangements for contact will be organised.

As described in Chapter 5, many agencies invite prospective adopters to attend panel when the match of a particular child with them is being considered. It would be good practice to consider doing that in these cases too, where the prospective adopters know the child, although language issues and distance could make it difficult. It is not likely to be feasible in other cases because, at this stage, the prospective adopters will have very little detailed information on the child.

What happens next?

The agency makes a decision in the usual way. It must then prepare a report on the child, compliant with Article 16 of the Convention. This report goes to the DfE which forwards it, via the foreign authorities, to the prospective adopters. If they decide to proceed, they travel to the UK to meet the local authority workers and the child. If both the local authority workers and the adopters want to proceed, the local authority must inform the DfE which will liaise with its counterpart in the adopter's country. An agreement to proceed is reached and arrangements can then be made for the placement to proceed. The child will usually be adopted in the adopter's country. However, before the child can leave the UK, he or she must live in the UK with the adopters for 10 weeks. They must then apply to the High Court for parental responsibility or for a Convention adoption order. Until one of these orders has been granted, they cannot leave the UK with the child (Adoption and Children Act ss.84 and 85).

The panel's involvement in children's cases when the Hague Convention is not in force in the overseas country

The child and his or her birth parents are counselled in the same way as for a Convention adoption.

The child's permanence report should include a summary of possibilities for placing the child within the UK and an assessment of whether adoption by a person in a particular overseas country is in the child's best interests, as is required for a Convention adoption.

Good practice suggests that the panel should consider whether the child should be placed for adoption in the overseas country as described for Convention adoptions.

In a non-convention case, the agency should send details of the proposed placement and its reasons for proposing the placement to the panel. In these cases, the child's agency will have arranged for the prospective adopter to be assessed and prepared in their own country. The assessment should usually be carried out in the individual's state of origin and be sent to the agency for consideration in the same way as for any other prospective adopter. The child's agency may have done some of this work itself and, exceptionally, may have done all the work. Panel members should consider the approval of the prospective adopters in the usual way.

The panel should consider the match as described for Convention adoptions. This will be followed by an agency decision and arrangements to place the child. The prospective adopters will need to confirm that both of them (or only one if the agency agrees) will accompany the child on leaving the UK. Before the child can leave the country, the prospective adopters must live with the child for 10 weeks and they must then apply for parental responsibility to the High Court. They are not able to take the child out of the country unless this has been granted (Adoption and Children Act 2002, ss.84 and 85).

Considering prospective adopters

Panel members should refer to Chapters 1, 2 and 4 as they have the same responsibilities when considering prospective intercountry adopters as they do when considering those who wish to adopt a child in the UK. The process for panel consideration, the agency decision-making and

the possible involvement of the IRM are the same, except that there are a few additional requirements in relation to prospective intercountry adopters.

The report on the prospective adopter must include:

(a) *the state of origin from which the prospective adopter wishes to adopt a child;*

(b) *confirmation that the prospective adopter is eligible to adopt a child under the law of that state;*

(c) *any additional information obtained as a consequence of the requirement of that state; and*

(d) *the agency's assessment of the prospective adopter's suitability to adopt a child who is habitually resident in that state.*

(FER 15(4) in relation to an adoption from a Convention country and very similar wording in AAR 25(6) in relation to a non-Convention country)

As for domestic adopters, the panel may give advice on the approval range for the prospective adopters. This will inform the agency's recommendation to the DfE once the agency has decided that the prospective adopters are suitable to adopt (AAR 30).

Although the same issues described in Chapter 4 should all be considered in relation to intercountry adopters, some are particularly significant for this group of prospective adopters and these are described below.

BAAF publishes a form which can be used to assess intercountry adopters – Form ICA.

Issues relating to the family

Age

UK adoption law does not specify an upper age limit for adopters. However, age is relevant and an important factor for consideration. The applicant or both partners should have a reasonable expectation of retaining good health to meet the demands of a child during their adolescence and through to adulthood.

Many countries do have explicit guidelines on age limits, both upper and lower, and on the age gap between adopters and child. These are some of the individual differences in a country's procedure on which the panel will require information.

Marital status

In England and Wales, any couple in a committed relationship can apply jointly to adopt, whether or not they are married and whether or not they are of the same or different sex. However, some countries overseas may have different requirements and it will be important that this is clarified in the report.

Criminal record

Apart from certain specified offences which automatically bar people from adopting, criminal convictions are taken into account by UK agencies but will not necessarily mean that prospective adopters are not approved. Some other countries, e.g. China, rule out most people with a criminal record. This needs to be clarified in the report.

Issues of culture, "race", religion and language

Many, though by no means all, children adopted from overseas into the UK will be brought up by adoptive parents who do not share the child's heritage in terms of culture, "race", religion or language. All children will have been separated not only from their birth family but also from their country of birth.

Prospective intercountry adopters will need to demonstrate that they have knowledge and understanding of the culture, religion and history of the country from which they propose to adopt and, if possible and realistic, some knowledge of the language. They will need to know, or be prepared to get to know, adults from that country who share their child's heritage and who are willing to take on the responsibility of a significant role in the child's life to help him or her to develop a positive self-image and take pride in their heritage. The prospective adopters will need to have some understanding of racism and a willingness to recognise and to deal with their child's need to handle racism. Where will they go for help with this? Panel members will need to enquire carefully into these issues, keeping in mind that standards applied in cases of intercountry adoptions should be as rigorous as those in domestic adoptions.

Range of children for whom applicants wish to be considered

Children are linked with adopters from overseas in the child's country of origin. However, regulations FER 4 and AAR 34 require the agency and the prospective adopters to share information on the child. The agency must meet and counsel the adopters about a possible placement of the child. They must be told about requesting an assessment for adoption support, and must be given the medical adviser's views on the likely health needs of the child.

When prospective adopters are applying in relation to a specific known child, probably a relative, as much information as possible about the child should be obtained by the agency. The assessment can then be focused on the prospective adopter's ability to meet that particular child's needs. In this situation the prospective adopter's report should name the child and give the date of birth. Approval will be in relation to that specific child.

Health considerations in relation to children

Many children for whom intercountry adoption is considered have been abandoned or placed in institutions by parents who provide little background or medical information about themselves or the child.

Prospective adopters need to be aware that there may well be as yet unknown genetic factors which will have considerable implications for the child. Are the applicants prepared and able to cope with uncertainties about the child's future development? How will they cope should medical conditions become apparent after placement? Children may also have been exposed to the risk of conditions such as tuberculosis, HIV infection, Hepatitis B and C, among others. Reliable and safe testing may not be available in the child's own country. How capable will adopters be of parenting a child who may have a serious medical condition? Children may have experienced abuse and neglect and severe physical, intellectual and emotional deprivation. Are prospective adopters prepared for this and for the long-term and perhaps permanent harm which may have been done? It is particularly important for panel members to enquire about these issues as some prospective intercountry adopters choose to adopt a child from overseas rather than from the UK because they want a child who will be both young and also relatively "straightforward" and problem-free. BAAF has produced a leaflet for intercountry adopters on these issues (see *Further Reading*).

The child's need for information

How aware are the applicants of the importance for children and young people of access to as much knowledge and information as possible about their birth family and the reasons for their placement? Do they understand the need to gather the information around the time of placement as this may be their only opportunity? Do they understand that the child's needs around this issue will change over time? How do they plan to meet these needs? Will they be able to help the child with his or her possible pain and anger that almost no information may be available? Do they view the lack of information and the unlikelihood of any possibility of contact with the child's birth family either now or in the future as a loss for the child and themselves or as a bonus? Sellick and Thoburn (1996) conclude in *What works in family placement?* that 'the successful adoptive parenting of children placed as infants is associated with the ability to accept the child's dual identity and the emotional significance which the family of origin will always have for the child and for themselves as substitute parents'.

Change of approval

Prospective adopters are approved as eligible and suitable to adopt a child from a specific country overseas. If the applicant wishes to apply to a different country after they are approved, there should be further discussion with the agency. An addendum report should be produced, which should evidence that the prospective adopter fully understands the cultural and other needs of a child from the "new" country. This report should be submitted to the adoption panel which should make a fresh recommendation. This will go, in the usual way, to the agency decision-maker for a new approval.

Post-placement and post-adoption support

Children coming from overseas for adoption in the UK are potentially very vulnerable and may have a range of special emotional, developmental, health and educational needs. They and their families may well need, and are entitled to be assessed for, post-placement and post-adoption support. What will be offered by the agency and how receptive is the family to this? Are the applicants in touch with any support groups, such as Adoption UK or a specialist group for intercountry adopters? (See Appendix 4.)

Reference

Sellick C and Thoburn J (1996) *What works in family placement?*, London: Barnardo's

Further reading

BAAF (2004) *Children Adopted from Abroad: Key health and developmental issues*, London: BAAF

BAAF (2004) *Intercounty Adoption: Information and guidance*, London: BAAF

Selman P (ed) (2000) *Intercountry Adoption: Developments, trends and perspectives*, London: BAAF

Appendix 1:
Context of the agency's placement work

It will be helpful for central list and panel members to have some factual information about the area that the agency covers and about both the general population and the children looked after by the local authority. The following list of questions provides a useful format for a brief report to be included in the pocket of the folder.

Local authorities

1) Information on the agency and the panel

- How many panels are there and what is their remit e.g. adoption only, adoption and permanence, fostering?
- Have the panel's roles and responsibilities changed recently?
- What volume of work does this panel deal with?
- Has this changed significantly in recent years?
- Are there any unusual aspects of the panel's work?

2) Information on the area served (much of this should be available in statistics produced from census information)

- What is the ethnic and cultural mix in the area?
- Are there areas which are unusual in terms of the ethnic and cultural mix within the area as a whole?
- What is the profile of the area in terms of:
  - the numbers of people with disabilities within the area?
  - employment/unemployment?
  - single parent families?
  - the housing mix?
  - youth justice issues?
  - poor school attendance?
  - general indices of poverty?
  - changes in population profile as a result of local government reorganisation?
- Do any localities stand out significantly in any of these respects?
- Have there been recent demographic changes?

3) Information on the children

- What is the percentage of children and young people in the population of the local authority as a whole?
- How many children are looked after?
- What percentage of children and young people in the general population of the local authority are looked after by the authority?
- How many of these are placed in local authority foster placements?
- How many are placed through independent fostering agencies?
- How many are in residential care?
- How many are in agreed long-term foster placements?
- How many are placed for adoption but not yet adopted?
- How many are identified as needing adoption or a permanent placement but not yet placed?
- How many looked after children became the subject of a residence order or a special guardianship order in the last year?

4) Information on foster carers

- How many foster carers does the agency have?
- How many of these are relatives of the child/young person placed?
- Is the pool of foster carers sufficient/insufficient to meet need?
- Are there particular groups of children/young people who are more difficult to place?
- Does the pool of short-term carers roughly equate in terms of ethnicity, culture, religion, language and class with the population of accommodated children and young people?
- Do the permanent carers approved through the panel roughly equate in terms of ethnicity, culture, religion, language and class with the population of looked after children and young people?

- Are the existing carers located close to the homes of the majority of the accommodated children and young people?

5) **Information on adopters**

- How many were approved last year
  - for domestic adoption?
  - for intercountry adoption?

- How many are approved and waiting for placements?

- How many have children in placement and not yet adopted?

Voluntary agencies

1) **Information on the agency and the panel**

- How many panels are there and what is their remit e.g. adoption only, adoption and permanence, fostering?

- Have the panel's roles and responsibilities changed recently?

- What volume of work does this panel deal with?

- Has this changed significantly in recent years?

- Are there any unusual aspects of the panel's work?

2) **Information about the area where the agency is located**

- Does the agency focus its activities mainly on this area?

- If not, what is the catchment area?

- Are there any geographical limitations?

- Do any geographical limitations relate solely to where referrals of children for family finding are accepted from or do they also relate to where referrals for potential families are accepted from?

3) **What is the focus of the agency's work?**

- Is there a particular specialism in terms of the kinds of children for whom the agency will family find?

- Is the agency contracted by a particular local authority to do specific work?

4) **Information on adopters**

- How many were approved last year
  - for domestic adoption?
  - for intercountry adoption?

- How many are approved and waiting for placements?

- How many have children in placement and not yet adopted?

Appendix 2:
Acts of Parliament, Statutory Instruments and Government Guidance

Acts	Abbreviations
The Adoption and Children Act 2002	
The Children Act 1989	The Children Act
The Data Protection Act 1998	

Statutory Instruments

Adoption Agencies Regulations 2005 SI 2005 no. 389	AAR
Adoption Agencies and Independent Review of Determinations (Amendment) Regulations 2011 SI 2011 no.589	
The Restriction on the Preparation of Adoption Reports Regulations 2005 SI 2005 no.1711	ARR
The Suitability of Adopters Regulations 2005 SI 2005 no.1712	SAR
The Adoption Support Services Regulations 2005 SI 2005 no.691	ASR
The Adoptions with a Foreign Element Regulations 2005 SI 2005 no.392	FER
The Special Guardianship Regulations 2005 SI 2005 no.1109	
The Fostering Services (England) Regulations 2011 SI 2011 no.581	The Fostering Regulations
The Adoption and Children Act 2002 (Commencement no.10 Transitional Savings and Provisions) Order 2005 SI 2005 no.2897	The Transitionals Order
The Children Act Representations Procedure (England) Regulations 2006 SI 2006 no.1738	The Complaints Regulations
The Care Planning, Placement and Case Review (England) Regulations 2010 SI 2010 no.959	The Review Regulations
The Local Authority Adoption Services (England) Regulations 2003 SI 2003 no.370	
The Adoption and Children (Miscellaneous Amendments) Regulations 2005 SI 2005 no.3482	

Government Guidance

Adoption Guidance – Adoption and Children Act 2002 revised in February 2011 by the DfE provides guidance for adoption agencies in England to the Adoption and Children Act 2002 and the Regulations and Court Rules. It was further revised in late April 2011.

Practice Guidance on Assessing the Support Needs of Adoptive Families (DfES, January 2005)

Practice Guidance on Preparing and Assessing Prospective Adopters (DfES, 2006)

Special Guardianship Guidance under the Children Act 1989 (DfES, May 2005)

The Children Act Guidance, Volume 4, *Fostering Services*

The Children Act Guidance, Volume 2, *Care Planning, Placement and Case Review*

Standards

National Minimum Standards for Adoption [local authorities and registered voluntary adoption agencies] (2011)

National Minimum Standards for Fostering (2011)

Appendix 3:
Glossary of terms

Accommodated/Accommodation

Under Section 20 of the Children Act 1989 the local authority is required to "provide accommodation" for children "in need" in certain circumstances. The local authority does not acquire parental responsibility (see below) merely by accommodating a child and the arrangements for the child must normally be agreed with the parent(s), who, subject to certain restrictions, are entitled to remove the children from local authority accommodation at any time.

Adoption placement plan

A plan that gives information to the prospective adopter about the child when the agency has decided to place the child with them. It sets out, for example, when the child will move into the prospective adopter's home, parental responsibility, adoption support services, contact with the child, and arrangements for reviewing the placement.

Adoption placement report

A report prepared by the adoption agency for the adoption panel which sets out, for example, the reasons for proposing the placement, arrangements for allowing any person contact with the child, the prospective adopter's view on the proposed placement, and, where the agency is a local authority, proposals for providing adoption support services for the adoptive family.

Adoption Register

A database of approved prospective adopters and children waiting for adoption across England and Wales. A team of experienced social workers will use the database to link children with approved prospective adopters where local matches cannot be found.

Adoption Support Agency (ASA)

An organisation or person registered, under Part 2 of the Care Standards Act 2000, to provide adoption support services. An ASA may operate on a profit or not-for-profit basis.

Article 15 report

Report prepared on the prospective adopter under Article 15 of the Convention on Protection of Children and Co-operation in respect of Intercountry Adoption (the Hague Convention). This includes information on their identity, eligibility and suitability to adopt, background, family and medical history, social environment, reasons for adoption, ability to undertake an intercountry adoption and the characteristics of the children for whom they would be qualified to care.

Article 16 information

Report prepared on the child under Article 16 of the Hague Convention. This includes information on his/her identity, adoptability, background, social environment, family history, medical history including that of the child's family, and any special needs of the child.

CAFCASS

The Children and Family Court Advisory and Support Service is a national non-departmental public body for England. It has brought together the services provided by the Family Court Welfare Service, the Guardian *ad Litem* Services and the Children's Division of the Official Solicitor. CAFCASS is independent of the courts, children's services, education and health authorities and all similar agencies.

CAMHS (Child and Adolescent Mental Health Services)

Services that contribute to the mental health care of children and young people, whether provided by health, education or children's services or other agencies. CAMHS cover all types of provision and intervention from mental health promotion and primary prevention, to specialist community-based services.

Care order

See "In care".

Care plan

An agreed plan for looking after a child and meeting that child's current and future needs, made by the placing authority under the Children Act 1989. The care plan will be presented to court when a care order is applied for.

Care proceedings

The court process involved in consideration of whether or not to make a care order.

Central list

Adoption agencies must set up a central list of people who must be checked, inducted and trained, and from which the members of each panel must be chosen. Fostering service providers must do the same thing in relation to fostering panels.

Children's guardian

A person working for CAFCASS who is appointed by the court to safeguard a child's interests in court proceedings.

Child's case record

A file that contains information about the child. This will include, for example, the child's permanence report, adoption panel's minutes, recommendation and advice given whether the child should be placed for adoption, agency decision, consent given or withdrawn, copy of placement order. The particular information to be kept is set out in AAR 12.1. and AIR 4.

Child's permanence report

A report prepared by the adoption agency. This will include, for example, information about the child and his/her family, a summary of the state of the child's health, his/her health history and any need for health care; wishes and feelings of the child, his/ her parent or guardian; the agency's view about the child's need for contact with his/her parents, guardian or any other person the agency considers relevant.

Child's review

Regulations prescribe that looked after children must have their care and the plans for them regularly reviewed. Reviews must happen, as a minimum, a month after the child starts being looked after, three months later, then every six months. Every major decision about a child should be considered at a review, including, clearly, the decision to start the adoption process.

Concurrent planning

This is the term given to a scheme in which children, usually babies or toddlers, for whom there is a chance that they might return home to their birth family, are placed with families who will foster them with this aim. However, the foster carers are also approved as adopters and will adopt the child should the planned return to the birth family not be successful. In this way, the moves that a child may otherwise have to make are minimised. These schemes have to be run with the agreement and co-operation of the local courts and to tight timescales.

Consortium

A group of usually not more than 6–8 local adoption agencies that share details of waiting families and children in order to try to make speedy local placements for children.

Contact/contact orders

Contact may be direct face-to-face contact between the child and another individual or it may be indirect, such as letters, often exchanged via the adoption agency by the child's adoptive parents and birth family members. This form of contact is often called letterbox contact. It is possible for a court to make a contact order requiring a specified form of contact, at the same time as or after the making of an adoption order. However, this is fairly rare.

Couple

Two people (whether of different sexes or the same sex) living as partners (married or unmarried) in an enduring family relationship. This does not include two people one of whom is the other's parent, grandparent, sister, brother, aunt or uncle.

CRB (Criminal Records Bureau)

An executive agency of the Home Office that provides access to criminal records and other information to organisations to help them make informed decisions. In the context of adoption, the CRB provides enhanced disclosures on prospective adopters and adult members of their household, which assist the adoption agency in their assessment of a prospective adopter's suitability to adopt a child. It also provides enhanced disclosures on panel members.

Decision-maker

A senior person within the agency who is a social worker with at least three years' post-qualifying experience in child care social work. The decision-maker makes the final decision, after considering the recommendation of the adoption panel and, in some cases, of the independent review panel. There may be more than one decision-maker but all must be qualified as above.

Fostering/foster care

In this book, this term is used for those cases where a child is placed with a foster carer approved by the local authority (under Section 23(2)(a) Children Act 1989) or (in rare cases) placed directly by a voluntary organisation (under Section 59 (1)(a) of the Act). These placements are governed by the Fostering Services Regulations 2002. "Short-term", "long-term", and "permanent" foster care and "respite care" (also known as "short breaks") may mean different things to different people; they are not legally defined terms.

In care

A child who is subject to a care order under Section 31 of the Children Act 1989 is described as being "in care". A care order gives the local authority parental responsibility for the child but does not deprive the birth parent(s) of this. Nevertheless, the local authority may limit the extent to which parents may exercise their parental responsibility and may override parental wishes in the interests of the child's welfare.

Independent Review Mechanism – Adoption & Fostering (IRM)

A review process that is conducted by an independent review panel. The prospective adopter may initiate this process when their adoption or fostering agency has made a qualifying determination. The review panel reviews the case and gives a fresh recommendation to the agency.

Independent Reviewing Officer (IRO)

Chairs statutory child care reviews for looked after children. He or she is independent of the child's social work team and of budget holders.

Looked after

This term includes both children "in care" and accommodated children. Local authorities have certain duties towards all looked after children and their parents, which are set out in Part III and Schedule 2 of the Children Act 1989. These include the duty to safeguard and promote the child's welfare and the duty to consult with children and parents before taking decisions.

Ofsted

The organisation responsible for registering adoption agencies and for inspecting adoption services every three years.

Open adoption

This term may be used very loosely and can mean anything from an adoption where a child continues to have frequent face-to-face contact with members of his or her birth family to an adoption where there is some degree of "openness" e.g. the birth family and adopters meeting each other once. People using the term should be asked to define what they mean!

Parental responsibility (PR)

All the rights, duties, powers, responsibilities and authority which by law a parent of a child has in relation to the child and his/her property. The most important elements of parental responsibility include:

- providing a home for the child;
- having contact with the child;
- protecting and maintaining the child;
- disciplining the child;
- determining and providing for the child's education;
- determining the religion of the child;
- consenting to the child's medical treatment;
- naming the child or agreeing to the child's change of name.

Placement order

An order made by the court under section 21 of the Adoption and Children Act 2002 authorising a local authority to place a child for adoption with any prospective adopters who may be chosen by the authority. It continues in force until it is revoked, or an adoption order is made in respect of the child, or the child marries, forms a civil partnership or attains the age of 18. Only local authorities may apply for placement orders.

Qualifying determination

In relation to *suitability to adopt a child* – a determination made by an adoption agency that it considers a prospective adopter is not suitable to be an adoptive parent and does not propose to approve him/her as suitable to be an adoptive parent.

Report on prospective adopter or Prospective adopter's report

A report prepared by the adoption agency.

- *Full report* – includes, for example, the prospective adopter's date of birth, identifying information, ethnic origin, cultural/linguistic background, religious persuasion, description of his/her personality, whether he/she is single or a member of a couple, the agency's assessment of his/her suitability to adopt a child, and a summary of the prospective adopter's state of health.
- *Brief report* – the agency does not need to complete a full report where it receives information that leads it to consider that the prospective adopter may not

be suitable to adopt a child. That information would be either that set out in Part 1, Schedule 4 of the AAR, or the health report, or report of interview with referees, or the local authority report, or other information.

Residence order

An order under Section 8 of the Children Act 1989 settling the arrangements as to the person(s) with whom the child is to live. Where a residence order is made in favour of someone who does not already have parental responsibility for the child (e.g. a relative or foster carer), that person will acquire parental responsibility subject to certain restrictions (e.g. they will not be able to consent to the child's adoption). Parental responsibility given in connection with a residence order will only last as long as the residence order. A residence order can last until the child's 18th birthday.

Residence order allowance

Local authorities have a power (under Schedule 1 Para 15 of the 1989 Children Act) to contribute to the cost of a child's maintenance when the child is living with somebody under a residence order provided he or she is not living with a parent or step-parent. A financial contribution under this power is normally referred to as a residence order allowance.

Special guardianship

A new order under the Adoption and Children Act 2002 offering an alternative legal status for children. The child is no longer looked after. It gives the special guardian parental responsibility which he or she can exercise to the exclusion of others. However, the birth parent(s) retain parental responsibility. Support services, including financial support, are very similar to those for adopters.

Twin-track, parallel or contingency planning

These are all names given to planning for a looked after child for adoption or long-term fostering while at the same time considering the possibility of placement with birth parents or with extended family members.

Appendix 4:
Useful organisations

British Association for Adoption & Fostering (BAAF)

The leading UK-wide organisation promoting best practice in both adoption and fostering services for children separated from their families. Its extensive publications are listed in a free catalogue or details are available on www.baaf.org.uk. Child placement consultants and trainers offer a phone and letter advice and information service and also provide training for panels and for social work teams. Family finding is provided by *Be My Parent*.

Head Office
Saffron House
6–10 Kirby Street
London EC1N 8TS
Tel: 020 7421 2600
Fax: 020 7421 2601
Email: mail@baaf.org.uk
www.baaf.org.uk

Be My Parent
as above
Tel: 020 7421 2666

BAAF Scotland
113 Rose Street
Edinburgh EH2 3DT
Tel: 0131 226 9270
Email: scotland@baaf.org.uk

BAAF Cymru
7 Cleeve House
Lambourne Crescent
Cardiff CF14 5GP
Tel: 029 2076 1155
Email: cymru@baaf.org.uk

BAAF Northern Ireland
Botanic House
1–5 Botanic Avenue
Belfast
BT7 1JG
Tel: 028 9031 5494
Email: northernireland@baaf.org.uk

BAAF England

Southern England
Saffron House
6–10 Kirby Street
London EC1N 8TS
Tel: 020 7421 2671
Email: southern@baaf.org.uk

Central England
Dolphin House
54 Coventry Road
Birmingham B10 0RX
Tel: 0121 753 2001
Email: midlands@baaf.org.uk

Northern England
MEA House, Ellison Place
Newcastle upon Tyne NE1 8XS
Tel: 0191 261 6600
Email: newcastle@baaf.org.uk

and at: Unit 4, Pavilion Business Park
Royds Hall Road
Wortley
Leeds LS12 6AJ
Tel: 0113 289 1101
Email: leeds@baaf.org.uk

Government departments

Department for Education
Floor 1, Sanctuary Buildings
Great Smith Street
London SW1P 3BT
Tel: 0870 000 2288
Email: info@dcsf.gsi.gov.uk
www.education.gov.uk

Department of Health Publications (DH)
Department of Health
PO Box 777
London SE1 6XH
Tel: 0300 123 1002
www.dh.gov.uk/publicationsandstatistics

Welsh Assembly Government
Children and Families Division
Cathays Park
Cardiff CF10 3NQ
Tel: 029 2082 3676
www.wales.gov.uk

Other organisations

Adoption UK
UK-wide self-help organisation for adoptive and
prospective adoptive parents. Produces lots of
helpful information, holds an Experience Resource
Bank, and publishes a newsletter, *Adoption Today*,
with useful articles and details of children waiting for
placement.
Linden House
55 The Green
South Bar Street
Banbury
Oxon OX16 9AB
Tel: 01295 752240
0844 848 7900 (helpline)
www.adoptionuk.org.uk

Family Rights Group (FRG)
A national organisation which advises families which
are in contact with children's services about the care
of their children.
The Print House
18 Ashwin Street
London E8 3DL
Tel: 020 7923 2628
www.frg.org.uk

Fostering Network
Produces a wide range of leaflets, publications and
training materials on all aspects of foster care and a
quarterly magazine.
87 Blackfriars Road
London SE1 8HA
Tel: 020 7620 6400
www.fostering.net

Independent Review Mechanism (IRM)
A review process, conducted by a panel, which
prospective adopters can use when they have been
told that their adoption agency does not propose to
approve them as adoptive parents.
Unit 4, Pavilion Business Park
Royds Hall Road
Wortley
Leeds LS12 6AJ
Tel: 0845 450 3956
www.irm-adoption.org.uk/

Intercountry Adoption Centre
Provides independent information and advice to
anyone in the UK considering adopting a child from
abroad, to adoptive families, adopted people and
adoption professionals.
64–66 High Street
Barnet
Herts EN5 5SJ
Tel: 0870 516 8742
www.icacentre.org.uk

Children and Families Across Borders
A voluntary organisation which helps families and
individuals whose lives are split between different
countries.
Unit 103
Canterbury Court
1–3 Brixton Road
London SW9 6DE
Tel: 020 7735 8941
Email: info@cfab.uk.net
www.cfab.uk.net

Natural Parents Network (NPN)
National self-help organisation for birth parents who
have parted with a child for adoption, run by birth
parents. Provides information, support and counsel
ling. Publishes a newsletter three times a year.
18 Bishops Way
Stradbroke
Eye
Suffolk IP21 5JR
Tel: 0845 456 5031
Email: administrator@n-p-n.co.uk
www.n-p-n.co.uk

Adults Affected by Adoption – NORCAP

National self-help organisation for adopted people, their birth relatives and adoptive families. Informative newsletter, contact leaders throughout the country, very helpful on all aspects of searching and can offer an intermediary service.
112 Church Road
Wheatley
Oxfordshire OX33 1LU
Tel: 01865 875000
www.norcap.org.uk

OASIS (Overseas Adoption Support and Information Service)

A UK-based voluntary support group for people who wish to adopt or who have already adopted children from overseas.
Contact them via their website:
www.adoptionoverseas.org

Post Adoption Centres

Organisations offering advice, counselling, information, training, and self-help and support groups to adopted people, birth families and adoptive families.

Adoption Support

Suite A, 6th Floor
Albany House
Hurst Street
Birmingham B5 4BD
Tel: 0121 666 6334
http://myweb.tiscali.co.uk/adoptionsupport/

Barnardo's Scottish Adoption Advice Service

Suite 5/3, Skypark SP5
45 Finnieston Street
Glasgow G3 8JU
Tel: 0141 248 7530
www.barnardos.org.uk/saas.htm

Birthlink (includes Adoption Contact Register for Scotland)

21 Castle Street
Edinburgh EH2 3DN
Tel: 0131 225 6441
www.birthlink.org.uk

After Adoption

Unit 5 Citygate
5 Blantyre Street
Manchester M15 4JJ
Tel: 0161 839 4932
Helpline: 0800 056 8578
www.afteradoption.org.uk

After Adoption has a number of regional offices around the UK

After Adoption – Yorkshire

Hollyshaw House
2 Hollyshaw Lane
Leeds LS15 7BD
Tel: 0113 230 2100 (advice line)
www.afteradoptionyorkshire.org.uk

Post-Adoption Centre

5 Torriano Mews
Torriano Avenue
London NW5 2RZ
Tel: 020 7284 0555
Email: advice@postadoptioncentre.org.uk
www.postadoptioncentre.org.uk

Introduction to Adoption: National Minimum Standards 2011

The NMS together with the adoption regulations form the basis of the regulatory framework under the Care Standards Act 2000 for the conduct of adoption agencies and adoption support agencies.

The values statement below explains the important principles which underpin these Standards.

Values – children

- The child's welfare, safety and needs are at the centre of the adoption process.

- Adopted children should have an enjoyable childhood, and benefit from excellent parenting and education, enjoying a wide range of opportunities to develop their talents and skills leading to a successful adult life.

- Children are entitled to grow up as part of a loving family that can meet their developmental needs during childhood and beyond.

- Children's wishes and feelings are important and will be actively sought and fully taken into account at all stages of the adoption process.

- Delays should be avoided as they can have a severe impact on the health and development of the children waiting to be adopted.

- A sense of identity is important to a child's well-being. To help children develop this, their ethnic origin, cultural background, religion, language and sexuality need to be properly recognised and positively valued and promoted.

- The particular needs of disabled children and children with complex needs will be fully recognised and taken into account.

- Where a child cannot be cared for in a suitable manner in their own country, intercountry adoption may be considered as an alternative means of providing a permanent family.

- Children, birth parents/guardians and families and adoptive parents and families will be valued and respected.

- A genuine partnership between all those involved in adoption is essential for the NMS to deliver the best outcomes for children; this includes the Government, local government, other statutory agencies, Voluntary Adoption Agencies and Adoption Support Agencies.

Values – adopted adults and birth relatives

- Adoption is an evolving life-long process for all those involved – adopted adults, and birth and adoptive relatives. The fundamental issues raised by adoption may reverberate and resurface at different times and stages throughout an individual's life.

- Adopted people should have access to information and services to enable them to address adoption related matters throughout their life.

- Agencies have a duty to provide services that considers the welfare of all parties involved and should consider the implications of decisions and actions for everyone involved.

- Agencies should seek to work in partnership with all parties involved, taking account of their views and wishes in decision-making.

- Agencies should acknowledge differences in people's circumstances and establish policies that provide non-discriminatory services.

- Adopted adults have their adoptive identity safeguarded and the right to decide whether to be involved in contact or communication with birth family members.

(Reproduced from Department for Education (2011) *Adoption: National Minimum Standards*, London: Department for Education. This information is licensed under the terms of the Open Goverment licence. Available at www.education.gov.uk)

Sample job description and person specification for central list and panel members

Job description

1. To read the circulated papers carefully before the meeting and to attend the meeting prepared to raise issues and to contribute to the panel discussion.

2. To take responsibility for participating in the making of a recommendation, on each case, drawing on both personal and professional knowledge and experience.

3. To attend meetings of the panel as specified in your agreement with the agency.

4. To be prepared to attend additional panels if possible, if requested.

5. To participate, with other members, in advising on policy and procedural matters as required.

6. To address diversity issues and promote anti-discriminatory practice.

7. To safeguard the confidentiality of all panel papers and panel discussions.

8. To participate in induction and training, which will be at least one day per year.

9. To participate constructively in the annual review of your central list and panel membership.

Person specification

Experience and qualifications

- Experience, either professionally or personally or both, of the placement of children in adoptive and foster families or of children being cared for away from their birth family.

- A social work or medical qualification will be necessary for certain panel members. The two social work members must have at least three years' post-qualifying experience in child care social work, including direct experience in adoption work.

Knowledge

- An appreciation of the effect of separation and loss on children.

- Awareness of the richness of different kinds of families and their potential for meeting children's needs.

- Some understanding of the purpose and function of the panel and of the agency which the panel is serving or a willingness to learn.

Abilities

- Good listening and communication skills.

- The ability to read, process and analyse large amounts of complex and sometimes distressing information.

- The ability to make an assessment and to form a view, based on the written and verbal information presented to panel, and the confidence to articulate this at panel.

- The ability to use personal and/or professional knowledge and experience to contribute to discussions and decision-making in a balanced and informed manner.

- The ability to work co-operatively as part of a multi-disciplinary team.

- The ability to attend panel meetings as required, arriving on time, and to attend at least one training day each year.

Attitudes and values

- A commitment to keeping children within their own family or community where this is possible and to maintaining contact between children living in adoptive families and their birth families where this appears to be in the child's best interest.

- A commitment to adoption as a way of meeting a child's need for permanence, where this appears to be in the child's best interests.

- A valuing of diversity in relation to issues of ethnicity, religion, gender, disability and sexuality.

- An understanding of, and a commitment to, the need for confidentiality.

- A willingness to increase knowledge and understanding of issues through reading, discussion and training.

- A willingness to contribute constructively to the annual review of your central list and panel memberships and, as required, to that of other panel members and the Chair.

Review of central list and panel members

Introduction

A review of the performance of all central list and panel members is required by statutory Guidance 1.35 and 1.36. This must happen at least annually and must be conducted by the agency adviser to the panel and the panel Chair. (See Chapter 1 for more information.)

An additional review could be convened, as required, by the agency or the member.

Preparation for the review

- The member should complete a self-evaluation form (see following page).

- The panel adviser and/or Chair should prepare a summary of any comments made by presenting social workers, service users or other panel members.

- Both the member and the agency adviser and Chair should check and reflect on the issues in the member's panel agreement (see section in Chapter 1) and on any job description and person specification which the member has had.

At the review

The member, the Chair and the panel adviser should meet and should go through and discuss

- the self-evaluation form

- the summary of comments made

- the panel agreement, and job description and person specification if applicable.

A written summary should be made and signed by the panel member, the Chair and the panel adviser.

After the review

The written summary and the supporting documents should be kept on the member's personnel file.

Sample self-evaluation form:
Central list and panel member

What do you think are your strengths as a panel member?

Is there anything you would like to change or improve in your performance as a panel member?

Do you have any suggestions about how this could be done?

Are there any factors which prevent you being as effective as you would like to be as a panel member?

Do you have any suggestions about how these could be addressed?

Is there any specific input or training which you would find helpful?

Do you have any comments about the general functioning of the panel or about the management of the central list?

Do you have any suggestions for how it could be improved?

Please comment on the strengths and any limitations of the Chair of the panel.

Please comment on the strengths and any limitations of any other panel members.

Signed: _____   Date: _____

Sample review form: central list and panel members

Date: **Name:**

Date of inclusion on the central list:

Dates or frequency of panels attended in the last year:

Strengths as a panel member

Areas for change and/or development by the panel member

How and by when will these be achieved?

Any changes to be made by the agency

How and by when will these be achieved?

Input and training planned

Signed central list/panel member: **Date:**

Agency adviser to the panel: **Date:**

Panel Chair: **Date:**

Sample job description and person specification for panel Chair

Job description

1. To chair panel meetings, ensuring that all items of business are covered and that the panel operates in accordance with Regulations and Guidance and the policies and procedures of the agency.

2. To prepare for panel meetings, reading panel papers carefully, identifying key issues and alerting the agency adviser if necessary to ensure, as far as possible, that the case is adequate for submission to panel.

3. To facilitate the active participate of all panel members in contributing to the panel's consideration of cases and to the making of clear and well-evidenced recommendations with the reasons for these.

4. To ensure that all those attending panel are treated with respect and courtesy.

5. To address diversity issues and to promote anti-discriminatory practice at all times.

6. To ensure that clear and accurate minutes are written, which record any serious reservations which panel members may have, and to be involved in checking and agreeing draft minutes with other panel members before they are sent to the decision-maker.

7. To liaise with the decision-maker and with other senior managers as required.

8. To ensure, with the agency adviser, that senior managers are aware of issues of concern, in relation both to individual cases and to more general matters.

9. To be involved as appropriate in the recruitment and appointment of central list and panel members and in any consideration about terminating the appointment of a member.

10. To review, with the agency adviser, the performance of central list and panel members as the need arises, and at least annually.

11. To assist in developing, promoting and monitoring policies and procedures and high standards of work in adoption and permanence services in the agency.

12. To assist in planning training for members and to participate in this at least one day per year.

13. To safeguard the confidentiality of all panel papers and panel discussions.

14. To be involved in:

- deciding whether a case is adequate for submission to panel;

- deciding on the attendance of observers at panel;

- deciding on the participation of a panel member who declares an interest in a case;

- deciding when an extra panel may be necessary;

- the preparation of an annual report on the panel's work.

Person specification

Experience and qualifications

- Experience, either professionally or personally or both, of the placement of children in adoptive and foster families and of children being cared for away from their birth family.

- Experience of chairing complex meetings.

Knowledge

- An appreciation of the effect of separation and loss on children.

- Awareness of the richness of different kinds of families and their potential for meeting children's needs.

- An understanding of the purpose and function of the panel and of the agency which the panel is serving.

- An understanding of the adoption process and of the legislative framework for the work of the panel, or the capacity to develop this knowledge quickly.

Abilities

- The authority and competence to chair a panel, ensuring that the business is covered and that the panel operates in accordance with Regulations, Guidance and the policies and procedures of the agency.

- Excellent interpersonal and listening skills.

- The ability to communicate well and clearly both verbally and in writing.

- The ability to process and analyse large amounts of complex and sometimes distressing information.

- The ability to identify key issues and possible solutions and to communicate these clearly.

- The ability to facilitate the active participation of all panel members in contributing to the panel's consideration of cases and recommendations.

- The ability to ensure that those attending panel are communicated with respectfully while also ensuring that panel members are able to explore any concerns they may have openly and honestly.

- The ability to manage the expression of strongly held but possibly conflicting views by panel members and to help the panel to reach a recommendation which takes account of all these views.

- The ability to take up issues as required with the agency, liaising with the decision-maker and other senior managers.

- The ability, working with the agency adviser, to review each central list and panel member's performance when required, and at least annually, ensuring that this is a helpful and constructive process for both the member and the panel as a whole.

Attitudes and values

- A commitment to keeping children within their own family or community where this is possible and to maintaining contact between children living in adoptive families and their birth families where this appears to be in the child's best interest.

- A commitment to adoption as a way of meeting a child's need for permanence, where this appears to be in the child's best interests.

- A valuing of diversity in relation to issues of ethnicity, religion, gender, disability and sexuality.

- An understanding of, and a commitment to, the need for confidentiality.

- A willingness to increase knowledge and understanding of issues through reading, discussion and training.

- A willingness to contribute constructively to the annual review of their role as panel Chair.

Review of panel Chair

Introduction

A review of the performance of the panel Chair is required by statutory Guidance 1.35 and 1.36. This must happen at least annually and must be conducted by the decision-maker. (See Chapter 1 for more information.)

An additional review could be convened, as required, by the decision-maker or the panel Chair.

Preparation for the review

- The panel Chair should complete a self-evaluation form (see overleaf)

- The panel adviser should prepare a summary of any comments made by presenting social workers, service users or other panel members.

- Both the panel Chair and the agency decision-maker should check and reflect on the issues in the Chair's panel agreement (see section in Chapter 1) and on any job description and person specification which the Chair has had.

At the review

The Chair and the decision-maker should meet and should go through and discuss

- the self-evaluation form

- the summary of comments made

- the panel agreement, and job description and person specification if applicable.

A written summary should be made and signed by the Chair and the decision-maker.

After the review

The written summary and the supporting documents should be kept on the Chair's personnel file.

Sample self-evaluation form: Panel Chair

What do you think are your strengths as a Chair?

- In panel meetings

- In your performance of the other responsibilities of the Chair

Is there anything you would like to change or improve in your performance as a Chair?

- In panel meetings

- In your performance of the other responsibilities of the Chair

Do you have any suggestions about how this could be done?

Are there any factors which prevent you being as effective as you would like to be as a panel Chair?

Do you have any suggestions about how these could be addressed?

Is there any specific input or training which you would find helpful?

Do you have any comments about the general functioning of the panel?

Do you have any suggestions for how it could be improved?

Signed: Date:

Sample review form: panel Chair

Date: **Name:**

Date of inclusion on the central list:

Dates or frequency of panels attended in the last year:

Strengths as a panel Chair

Areas for change and/or development by the panel Chair

How and by when will these be achieved?

Any changes to be made by the agency

How and by when will these be achieved?

Input and training planned

Signed panel Chair: **Date:**

Agency decision-maker: **Date:**

Checklist of additional information which may be provided by the agency

Please tick if included

☐ List of central list members (with brief details and email addresses/phone numbers)

☐ Name, job title and email address/telephone number of the professional adviser

☐ Name and job title of the agency decision-maker

☐ Central list and panel agreement for members

☐ Format for undertaking the annual review of central list and panel members

☐ Context of the agency's placement work (see Appendix I)

☐ The latest annual report of the panel, if one is produced

☐ The latest management report detailing activity levels in the agency's adoption work

☐ The latest set of policy and procedures for adoption work, prepared under Regulation 7 of the Adoption Agencies Regulations 2005

☐ Any other relevant policies not included in the above

☐ Arrangements for considering long-term fostering situations

☐ Information on the assessment and preparation process for applicants, including the programme for groups

☐ Relevant extracts from Children's Services Plan

☐ Child care or permanence policy

☐ Equal opportunities policy

☐ Child Protection policy

Any other information

☐

☐

☐

Book list

Adoption stories

Real-life stories written by adopters who have experienced the highs and lows of adoption at first hand.

An Adoption Diary, by Maria James

A true story of an adoption, following Maria's and Rob's journey to adopting a two-year-old child, and the highs and lows along the way.

Flying Solo, by Julia Wise

Inspiring and accessible, this book describes the realities of life on your own with an adopted child, with practical hints and tips.

In Black and White, by Nathalie Seymour

This honest account follows a white couple living in 1970s Britain who adopted two black children, describing how the children settle in, get to know their birth relatives and eventually decide to leave their adoptive home.

Together in Time, by Ruth and Ed Royce

From a dual perspective, the authors look back on their decision to adopt a boy with attachment difficulties, the fear that their family was falling apart, their experience of music and art therapy, and their decision to adopt for a second time.

The Family Business, by Robert Marsden

A revealing story of the adoption of William, a little boy with cerebral palsy, by a middle-aged couple with three birth children, and the effects on their family life.

Adoption Undone, by Karen Carr

The true story of an adoption and an adoption breakdown, bravely told by the adoptive mother as she looks back at what went wrong and why.

Take Two, by Laurel Ashton

This candid account reveals the author's personal heartache at her infertility, the emotional and physical demands of IVF; how and why the decision to adopt two young girls is the right choice for this family in waiting.

I wish I had been Born from You, by Karen Lomas

Written by a mother, with contributions from her adopted daughter, this heartfelt collection charts a moving and emotional adoption journey of getting to know one another and becoming a family.

Frozen, by Mike Butcher

Written by an adoptive father, this honest and humorous account explores the lengths to which one couple are pushed to create their dream of a family. It provides a shocking exposure of how IVF treatment can go horribly wrong and reveals how a flyer from an adoption agency changes the couple's life.

When Daisy met Tommy, by Jules Belle

The story of how six-year-old Daisy and her parents adopted Tom. Although written by her mother, Daisy's thoughts and feelings about the family's decision to adopt, and her perspective on the process, are vividly brought to life.

Is it True you have Two Mums?, by Ruby Clay

The heart-warming story of Ruby and Gail and their belief in their potential to adopt. Some social workers they encounter think that, as a lesbian couple, they are unfit to be parents; others recognise that their Asian dual-heritage family has much to offer. This account charts their journey to becoming parents to three adopted daughters.

Becoming Dads, by Pablo Fernández

Set against a contemporary backdrop of diverse perceptions – both encouraging as well as hostile – as to whether gay men should adopt, Pablo's narrative tracks their journey, from their own initial doubts about whether or not they would be accepted, through to the positive affirmations they receive and their adoption of a young boy.

As if I was a Real Boy, by Gordon and Jeannie Mackenzie

The inspirational story of how Gordon, who was 10 and living in a psychiatric hospital with undiagnosed mental health issues, was adopted by Jeannie. In a moving account, mother and son look back at how adoption changed their lives for the better.

Anthologies

Adopters come together to share their experiences.

Loving and Living with Traumatised Children, by Megan Hirst

Based on the experiences of nine individuals who adopted traumatised children, this book looks at the "co-operative enquiry" they set up to investigate the effects of trauma on themselves.

Could you be my Parent?, edited by Leonie Sturge-Moore

An inspiring and informative collection of accounts of various aspects of adoption and fostering as published in BAAF's family-finding newspaper *Be My Parent*.

Looking After our Own, edited by Hope Massiah

This inspiring collection looks at the experiences of nine adoptive families and their children, exploring their motivation to adopt, what their social workers had to offer or not, the roles of friends and family, and what adoption has meant to them.

Adopters on Adoption, by David Howe

This absorbing collection of personal stories gives an insider's description of the growth of adopted children into adulthood. Experienced adopters (whose children are now young adults) describe the importance and distinctiveness of adoptive parenting.

Adoption guides

Advice Note: Intercountry Adoption

This short guide describes the intercountry adoption process and includes: information on the reasons it is sometimes used; some of the issues and implications for families involved; and basic practical guidance on procedures and rules.

Adoption Conversations, by Renée Wolfs

This in-depth practical guide explores the questions adopted children are likely to ask, with suggestions for helpful explanations and age-appropriate answers. Although the guide focuses primarily on the needs of children adopted from abroad, the practical advice is applicable to any adopted child.

Approaching Fatherhood, by Paul May

The first book in the UK to combine adoptive fathers' experiences with a guide to the adoption process – from the man's point of view. This book examines who these adoptive dads are, how they tick, and what they make of the families they create.

More Adoption Conversations, by Renée Wolfs

This in-depth practical guide explores the problems that adopted teenagers (up to 18 years old) are likely to confront and provides suggestions for helpful solutions and achievable communication methods.

The Pink Guide to Adoption for Lesbians and Gay Men, by Nicola Hill

This essential step-by-step guide, the first of its kind to be published in the UK, explores the adoption process and examines how being a prospective lesbian or gay adopter can and does affect every aspect of this. Illustrated throughout with quotations and true stories.

Related by Adoption, by Hedi Argent

This new and comprehensively revised edition of BAAF's popular handbook gives grandparents-to-be and other relatives information about adoption today, how it will affect them, and the positive roles they can play.

Talking about Adoption, by Marjorie Morrison

This popular and comprehensive guide outlines the whys, whens and hows of telling the truth about an adopted child's origins, based on the experiences of many people who have been adopted, and adopted parents.

By adopted children and adults

What do children think about adoption? How do adopted adults feel their lives have been affected?

The Colours in Me, edited by Perlita Harris

A unique collection of poetry, prose and artwork by adopted children and young people. Over 80 contributors – ranging from four to 20 years of age – tell it like it is, revealing what it feels like and what it means to be adopted.

Readings from The Colours in Me DVD

Filmed on location at The Drill Hall in London, this inspirational and thought-provoking DVD features readings by 30 children and young people who contributed to BAAF's popular anthology *The Colours in Me*.

Special and Odd, by James Mulholland
In this revealing and extraordinarily witty memoir James Mulholland tells the story of how he met his birth mother 29 years after being given up for adoption.

Mother Me, by Zara H Phillips
In this intensely personal and compelling memoir, Zara H Phillips examines her relationships with her adoptive and birth mothers, and invites the reader to join her in her own journey to become a mother.

Just a Member of the Family DVD
This is the first film about adoption from a child's point of view, and features a number of birth children talking about how they were prepared and prepared themselves for an adopted child joining the family.

Handbooks

The Attachment Handbook for Foster Care and Adoption, by Gillian Schofield and Mary Beek
This comprehensive and authoritative book provides an accessible account of core attachment concepts, enabling readers to understand the kind of caregiving in foster and adoptive families that can help children to feel more trusting, confident, competent and secure.

A Child's Journey through Placement, by Vera Fahlberg
Separation, loss, grief and change are experiences common to children requiring permanent placements. This essential reference book contains the theoretical knowledge base and skills necessary for understanding, working with, and planning for these children and their families.

The Child Placement Handbook, edited by Gillian Schofield and John Simmonds
This authoritative collection captures a wealth of knowledge and wisdom across diverse child placement issues, from the impact of abuse and neglect prior to placement to the challenges of providing support.

From the Ten Top Tips series

A series that looks at some fundamental issues in adoption, with the inclusion of some good practice points.

Making Matches, by Jennifer Cousins
Considers the needs of both children and adults, how these impact on the matching process and how a balance in meeting both can be maintained, with an emphasis on clarifying the issues and developing practice.

Placing Children, by Hedi Argent
Explores the issue of child placements, with an emphasis on evidence from practice and experiences, with clear and concise accounts of what works and what does not.

Placing Siblings, by Hedi Argent
Explores the different, often conflicting, principles involved in placing looked after siblings, including when to keep siblings together or help them to part; listening to each child and getting to know the group; and using kinship care.

Supporting Adopters, by Jeanne Kaniuk with Eileen Fursland
Describes the legal framework for adoption support and the principles on which a successful support service depends, along with information on financial support, supporting the wider family, managing children's difficult behaviour and contact.

Good Practice Guides

Every Child is Special, by Jennifer Cousins
Looks at placing disabled children for permanence, including the recruitment and assessment of families, assessing and profiling children, linking and matching, and supporting families.

Recruiting, Assessing and Supporting Lesbian and Gay Carers and Adopters, by Gerald P Mallon and Bridget Betts
Explores how agencies can work effectively and successfully to recruit, assess and support lesbian and gay applicants, with consideration of the policy and practice issues.

Recruiting Black and Minority Ethnic Adopters and Foster Carers, **by Gwen Rule**
Looks at how agencies can work effectively to recruit black and minority ethnic applicants, covering the factors stopping carers from coming forwards, the impact of racism, how to prepare and support carers, and recruitment policy and planning.

Right from the Start, **by Jennifer Cousins**
Looks at best practice in adoption planning for babies and very young children.

Together or Apart?, **by Jenifer Lord and Sarah Borthwick**
Highlights factors which affect decisions on whether siblings are placed together or separately, and considers when, how and by whom key decisions are made.